D0028280

"Many writers have touched on the nature of the call of God, and many preachers have exhorted Christians to respond to the call of God. But seldom has anyone provided an articulate and clearly understood explanation of what the call of God is. As a pastor, denominational leader, and seminary president, Jeff Iorg has counseled with many regarding God's call. His book *Is God Calling Me?* will be a valuable resource for anyone seeking to discern God's call. Acknowledging all believers have a call of God on their lives, Iorg effectively categorizes the more specific calls to Christian leadership or missionary service as well as God's call to a particular job or location. His review of the diverse ways God calls will dispel doubts and indecision while giving assurance and confidence to many."

 — **Jerry Rankin,** President
 International Mission Board

"Reading *Is God Calling Me?* is the next best thing to sitting on the porch and discussing this pivotal life question with a wise mentor. If you are unable to engage in the latter, I strongly recommend that you read this down-to-earth book. It could change your life!"

 — **Ron Ellis,** President
 California Baptist University

"This book needed to be written. Dr. Iorg speaks as a pastor and theologian as he tackles the question that every Christian leader has asked: 'Is God calling me?' This is a must-read for every seminary student, potential missionary, or pastor-to-be."

— **Geoff Hammond,** President
  North American Mission Board

"Practical and thought provoking, *Is God Calling Me?* by Dr. Jeff Iorg is a wonderfully insightful book of benefit for a new generation of Christian leaders. What an excellent tool for collegiate ministry!"

— **Linda H. Osborne**
  National Collegiate Ministry Leader
  LifeWay Christian Resources

"Dr. Jeff Iorg is right on! *Is God Calling Me?* is concise, clear, and inspiring. I recommend it to anyone seeking insight to ministry. My heartfelt thanks to Dr. Iorg's personal illustrations and openness; it was refreshing."

— **Rob Zinn,** Senior Pastor
  Immanuel Baptist Church,
  Highland, California

"What an incredible book to help you understand God's calling on your life. Anyone seeking God's will can find significant assistance here."

— **Max Barnett,** Christian Challenge Director
  State of Colorado

IS GOD CALLING ME?

jeff
iorg

IS GOD CALLING ME?

answering the question
every believer asks

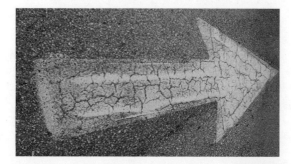

PUBLISHING GROUP
Nashville, Tennessee

© 2008 by Jeff Iorg
All rights reserved
Printed in the United States of America

ISBN: 978-0-8054-4722-4

Published by B&H Publishing Group,
Nashville, Tennessee

Dewey Decimal Classification: 253.2
Subject Heading: LEADERSHIP \ GOD—WILL
PASTORAL WORK

Unless otherwise noted, all Scripture quotations are taken from the
Holman Christian Standard Bible® Copyright © 1999, 2000, 2002,
2003 by Holman Bible Publishers. Used by permission. Holman
Christian Standard Bible®, Holman CSB®, and HCSB® are federally
registered trademarks of Holman Bible Publishers.

3 4 5 6 7 8 9 10 11 12 13 14 15 16   13 12 11 10 09

For my children—
Casey, Melody, and Caleb—
And the generation of young leaders they represent.
We need your passion.

Take over.

Contents

A Conversation about the Question

You probably selected this book because you are try-ing—maybe even struggling—to answer the ques-tion on the cover: "Is God calling me?" Considering this question reveals something very positive about your spiri-tual sensitivity and commitment. Answering it will deter-mine your spiritual destiny.

"Is God calling me?" is *the essential question* you must answer before entering ministry leadership or accepting a specific ministry assignment. Settling the issue of call is foundational to effective Christian leadership. Being "called" is one characteristic of distinctly *Christian* leader-ship. Answering this question, initially, charts a lifelong course of ministry leadership. Knowing how to answer the question subsequently, at key junctures in life, will clarify God's assignment of specific leadership roles or responsibilities. "Is God calling me?" is a question you must answer now and be able to answer again and again over a lifetime.

As ministry leaders, we serve in response to God's invitation and at his pleasure, not at our initiative. Throughout the Bible and church history, men and women have responded to God's call and led his people. The demands of ministry leadership are simply too great and the consequences too long lasting to assume these roles capriciously or casually. Ministry leadership is a calling we answer, not a career we pursue.

You may be struggling to answer this question, confused by the different perspectives you have heard and frustrated by the many ways people describe the concept of call. If so, take heart! You share a common struggle almost every Christian leader experiences. I hope this book will help you solve the problem without adding to your frustration.

The insights in this book have been hammered out over more than thirty years of personally pursuing God's call and many years of teaching others to do the same. Students and conference participants have heard my messages and presentations on God's call and have freely critiqued me. Sometimes, they changed my mind. Other times, they helped me think more critically and communicate more clearly. Sharpening this message has been a fulfilling, but sometimes painful, quest.

What you are about to read is not an exhaustive treatment of God's call. It is, however, a collection of field-tested insights that have helped many to clarify their understanding of call. Others have, and will, write longer books on God's call. My first goal is to cut straight to the heart of the matter and give you tools to work through the call process. But detailed analysis and intellectual understanding are not enough. My ultimate goal for you is clarity about God's call so you can answer affirmatively! If God is calling you, obedience is the only desired response.

My prayer is that God's call will become crystal clear and his grace will empower and motivate you to radical obedience. God is calling out a new generation of passionate leaders—kingdom leaders—who will accelerate the fulfillment of the Great Commission in this generation. Perhaps you are one of them. As you read, ask God for insight and spiritual discernment. Your future and the future leadership of the kingdom of God are in the balance. The stakes are high, but God's power and grace are sufficient to call you and sustain you in ministry leadership.

May God inspire and direct you as you read!

Defining the Concept of Call
CHAPTER 1

Few concepts are talked about more and understood less in Christian circles than God's call. Some believers claim to be called into ministry, to missions, to the pastorate, or to some other church leadership role as a special instruction from God. Others contradict that narrow understanding with the claim that all believers are equally called to serve God. Still others point out phrases in the Bible such as "called to be holy" or "called out of darkness" (i.e. 1 Pet. 1:15, 2:9) as evidence that calling is just another word for a common spiritual experience, not a special or specific instruction from God.

Who is right about all this? Does God call people to serve him in special ways? Are all believers called? If they are, are all callings equal before God? Is the concept of call simply another way to describe the sanctification process?

Is it an overspiritualized way to describe how circumstances just happened to turn out? Or does all this fit together somehow as these definitions and understandings relate to one another?

Part of the problem in understanding the concept of call is the different ways *call* is used in popular vernacular. The most common is a phone call. More than 200 million Americans own cell phones. People can call almost anyone, anytime. *Call* can also mean to speak in a loud voice, to summon attention. It can mean a distinct sound—like a mating call.

Call describes inviting someone to participate on a team, join a program, or do their duty. For example, a player is called up from the junior varsity to the varsity, or a reservist is called to active military service, or a citizen is called for jury duty. You might also call for an investigation or call for the question or call for a hand to be shown in cards. The instructions at a square dance are called. A football announcer calls a game, and a tennis match can be called off when it rains.

An umpire calls a game, and a loan officer can call in a bad loan. You are supposed to call a spade a spade, call the shots when you are in charge, and call it quits at the end of the day. And when a friend is bereaved, you call on them to pay your respects.

No wonder there is so much confusion! The word *call* is overworked, shaped by its context to fit multiple definitions and situations. The word means so many things, it is difficult to isolate a core definition.

There are, however, two recurring themes throughout these different usages of *call*. First, a call brings new information. When your phone rings, someone usually wants to tell you something. Whether you call a game or call for the question, you are communicating. So, a call transmits new information. Second, a call brings new responsibility. A call puts you on the team, into battle, or on a jury. You are called to do something—play a game, dance a jig, make a decision. A call means it's your turn to get involved.

Keep these two ideas in mind—information and responsibility—as we develop an understanding of God's call. As we move toward a biblical understanding of call, these two concepts will be important. When God calls, he gives new information about how to live. When he calls, he assigns new responsibility in his kingdom.

Unfortunately, when used in Christian circles, there are almost as many different uses for the word or concept of *call* as in popular vernacular. We label all kinds of experiences "a call from God." We use the word to describe different kinds of spiritual experiences with little regard for precise meanings. We say we are called and presume the context helps our hearers know what we are talking about. Sometimes that works. Too often, however, people smile and nod—confused about what we are talking about but too polite to question or contradict us.

Writers on the subject of call have contributed to this problem. A survey of the literature reveals many pages devoted to describing call experiences, defending the importance of a call, trying to explain what it is, and encouraging people to clarify and honor their call. All this, but seldom can you find a one-sentence definition of *call* that is consistently explained, used, and interpreted.

This book is different. After considering dozens of call experiences in the Bible, reflecting on my own experiences of being called, listening to other leaders describe their unique call stories, and reading many books and articles on call—here is my definition:

> *A call is a profound impression from God*
> *that establishes parameters for your life and can be altered*
> *only by a subsequent, superseding impression from God.*

A Call Is a Profound Impression from God

A call is an inner experience. It is an impression from God, an inner experience with God. It is a work of the heart. A call is something you know you have, you are confident is real, and yet it is often difficult to quantify or explain. You know you are called, in short, because you know it in your heart.

This experience-based definition troubles some people. Certainly such an important spiritual concept must be more objective than this. Allowing this much subjectivity might lead to abuse, misunderstanding, false claims, and uncertainty. Absolutely! The issue of call is open to all kinds of misinterpretations and mistakes. But that does not mean the definition is incorrect. It simply means we must learn to discern God's call by shaping our thinking with the Bible and evaluating our experience in its context and under its authority. A call *is* a subjective experience with God but always set against a biblical backdrop.

Observing the response of some seminary students to this point is amusing. They analyze everything, looking for concrete answers. So, after surveying the biblical material and critically analyzing the literature, it troubles some when I say, "When it comes to being called, ultimately, you just know it in your heart." There is no definitive three-step formula for understanding or experiencing God's call. Being called is more intuitive than analytic no matter how much data you collect (*or* how systematically this book tries to explain God's call). No amount of reasoning replaces the heartfelt conviction that God is calling you.

A call is a *profound* impression. A common practice in Christian circles is to use several terms interchangeably to describe an experience of God's direction. These include prompting, leading, directing, showing, and urging. For example, we say, "God prompted me . . . God led me . . . God directed me . . . God is showing me . . . God gave me a special desire to . . ." and so on. All of these are valid expressions. They are all ways we try to communicate the inner sense that God is guiding us.

But none of these terms should be used to describe a call. A call is different from a prompting, leading, directing, showing, or urging from God. A call is a *profound* impression from God. It is more than what happens routinely through daily devotions or daily discernment of God's activity in and through our lives. A call is a rare event. A call impacts us profoundly. A call resonates deeply within us and has long-lasting results.

As I'm writing this, I have been a believer in Jesus Christ for thirty-five years. My personal relationship with God through Jesus began when I was thirteen years old. Since then, I have had only five call experiences with God. Five call experiences in thirty-five years as a disciple! As we move through this book, I will use those experiences and the experiences of others to illustrate different aspects of the concept of call. But for now, remember this key point: call experiences are unique, infrequent encounters with God.

During my thirty-five years following God, he has prompted me, led me, directed me, shown me his will, and urged me in specific directions many times. I sense God's direction as I counsel people about spiritual issues, handle administrative matters, determine where and what to preach or teach, and manage the multiple demands of my ministry and family. All of these are valid experiences, but they are *not* callings.

A call is a profound impression from God. It happens rarely and has significant, life-altering ramifications. A call is an inner impression boring into the core of your soul, changing you forever. It is a deep inner work, sometimes an emotional, heartrending encounter with God. A call often unsettles or overturns life, while at the same time producing deep inner peace or satisfaction. On the outside, life may be disrupted. On the inside, you have a settled assurance of God's will. You cannot really explain it better than to say, "I'm called . . . and I know it in my heart." And, when you know you are called, you live with its implications and the full impact of its meaning in your life.

A Call Establishes Parameters for Your Life

A call establishes parameters—protective guides—that bracket your life. Like giant parentheses, a calling establishes barriers to protect you and guide your behavior. A calling means you say yes to some things and no to others. When God calls, life's choices must be made in the context of answering the call. Anything incompatible with obedience must be rejected in pursuit of the call.

For example, God called me to ministry leadership prior to meeting my wife Ann. When we started dating, we had to settle an important issue quite early in our relationship. I could not date anyone who did not have a similar call to ministry leadership (and it turned out Ann had the same conviction). We discovered we shared a similar calling. This did not mean we were going to get married, but it gave us both the freedom to pursue our relationship, knowing marriage was possible.

Several college students have told me painful stories of ending relationships with potential life partners who did not share their call. One woman told me, "God has called me to give my life in China. Leaving my boyfriend over that issue was the single hardest decision I have ever made." A young man sobbed deeply as he told of being dumped by his high-school sweetheart after God called him during college to be a pastor.

These parameters are not just relational. One friend reported, "God has called me to be a bivocational pastor, so I cannot accept offers from larger churches who would pay me a full-time salary." When his church grew, he added other staff members rather than becoming a full-time pastor. A missionary was interviewed for a faculty position at a seminary but withdrew from the process, saying, "God called me to be a missionary, not to teach missions. I just can't leave the field." Another person turned down lucrative secular employment, saying, "My call is to full-time ministry leadership. No distractions or temptations allowed." All of these people recognize different but very real parameters put in place by their call from God.

A clear sense of call means more than saying no. It also informs our yeses. A college student reported, "God has called me to teach public school—my passion is junior-high kids!" So she is in college preparing to pursue God's call. A veteran pastor recently resigned a twenty-year pastorate to return to seminary. Why? God has called him to teach in the last season of his ministry, and additional academic preparation is required by those new parameters. Your calling establishes parameters—giant parentheses around your life—that control your choices and direct the outcome of your life.

This can be difficult for other people to understand. Parents struggle when their children answer a call to international missions. They wonder, "Can't you just do your ministry with immigrants in our country?" Yet, a person called to take the gospel to another place must go. Family members can also question a call when it comes later in life. Many people today are answering God's call to ministry after years in secular careers. Children accustomed to a certain lifestyle question their parents and wonder why they would forgo lucrative employment to enter the ministry. The answer is simple: the call mandates the change.

A call from God establishes parameters—parentheses, barriers, guidelines—that determine your choices in the future. What fits within the parameters of the call is acceptable; what does not is not. God-called people find contentment within these barriers. One wise mission leader said, "The safest place to be, anywhere in the world, is in the center of God's call." God uses the parameters of your call to place you where he wants you, to protect you while you accomplish his purposes, and to shape you for effective service.

A Call Can Be Changed Only by Another Call

Because a call is a profound impression with lasting results, it will not be amended or added to very often. A call is an infrequent experience. When you are called, you stay called! But most Christian leaders experience a series of callings in their lives. The next chapter describes this process and explains a model for understanding the unfolding experience of God's callings.

This *flexible-permanence* of God's call means, when God calls, you remain faithful to the call until he calls again. Sometimes Christian leaders speak of being "released from a call." That does not seem to be an accurate explanation of how God works. In the Bible, God always called people *to* someone, something, or somewhere. His calls were proactive, leading people to do new things, go new places, or attempt new ministries. A release from a prior call happens because a subsequent, superseding call experience overrides the previous call.

This understanding of call has two implications. First, God-called people pursue ministry as a calling, not as a ministry career. Your goal is not a bigger position, higher paycheck, or more prestigious situation. You are called, so you serve to fulfill your calling. Second, being called means you persevere through tough times. God-called men and women do not quit when circumstances are difficult. God-called people stay put, firmly planted, until they receive a subsequent, superseding call to a new assignment from God.

Ministry leaders, like secular employees, receive offers to change jobs. A pastor might be asked to leave one church for another, or a missionary could be asked to change people groups or mission fields. In these situations, ministry leaders do not make their decisions primarily based on compensation, benefit to family, suitability for service, or the ripeness of the opportunity. They make their decisions based on call.

The proper question to ask when offered a different assignment must be "Is God calling me to this new role?" When I interview any person for a ministry position, I always ask them to describe how they are experiencing God's call regarding the position. I am not listening for a formulaic answer, but I want to hear how a person is pursuing God and listening for his call. Taking a ministry position is not like taking a secular job. You must be called, not just employed.

A call is a profound impression from God that establishes parameters for your life and can be altered only by a subsequent, superseding impression from God. A call brings new information and new responsibility. A call is more than a prompting or leading; it is a life-changing experience with God. A call is an inner reality, difficult to quantify but nonetheless real. Although defining a call is helpful to understanding the concept, learning the definition is not the objective. When you are called, when you *know* you are called, nothing short of an obedient response is acceptable!

Three Types of Call Experiences

CHAPTER 2

Although the word *call* is used in many ways in popular culture and in Christian vernacular, the Bible uses the term in three distinct ways. These usages describe three types of callings—one experienced by every believer and the other two reserved for people called to ministry leadership. Discovering the distinction between these aspects of God's call clarifies and simplifies this oft-confusing subject.

These three different call experiences are distinct but related to one another. Our lives (and our callings) are a series of experiences, each one intertwined with the next to create life's tapestry. A calling often emerges from a previous call experience and its results. One layer of call creates the framework for the next to unfold. These experiences cascade from one another, building upon one another and flowing through our lives. Callings connect like the sections of a collapsible telescope—as it is pulled apart, sections emerge from other sections until it is assembled and useful. Similarly, God's calls emerge from universal to specific, from previous to current, building on the past and completing the whole.

There are three distinct aspects of God's call. We are not talking here about the ways God calls; we'll save that for another chapter. This chapter is about the kinds or types of calls you may experience. First, there is a *universal call* to Christian service for all believers. Second, there is a *general call* of some believers to ministry leadership, sometimes popularly (though incorrectly) equated with paid ministerial employment. Third, there is a *specific call* to a unique ministry assignment or a particular ministry position. Let's consider each of these calls and how it relates to the overall concept of call.

A Universal Call to Christian Service and Growth

God calls every believer to Christian service. This call includes not only serving others but also personal growth resulting in changed behavior (what the Bible calls *sanctification*). Paul wrote, "Walk worthy of the calling you have received" and then listed character and behavioral expectations of believers (Eph. 4:1–3). Peter echoed the same idea, writing, "As the One who called you is holy, you also are to be holy in all your conduct" (1 Pet. 1:15). Both of these men filled their letters with reminders that believers are called to walk in the light, be holy, live for God's glory, and enjoy freedom in Christ.

God has called you to live differently from people around you and differently from how you lived prior to conversion. You are called to a new way of life. God has given you new information and responsibility to live for him. This call, this profound impression from God, was part of your conversion experience (note the past tense of the verbs in the Scriptures quoted above). Your conversion included your call to Christian service and growth.

Though you may not have fully understood your called-out status at your conversion, that does not invalidate the reality of the experience. You were also sealed by the Spirit for eternal life (Eph. 1:13), baptized by the Spirit into the universal church (1 Cor. 12:13), and gifted by the Spirit for special service in the church (1 Cor. 12:1–11). These and many other blessings and responsibilities happened at the moment of your conversion. Regardless of whether or not you fully understood all of these experiences, they all happened—including your call to Christian service and growth.

One important aspect of God's universal call is how it relates to a Christian's employment or vocation. If God has called every believer to serve him, does that mean every believer should be employed full-time in some form of Christian ministry? Should every believer quit his or her job and devote every waking hour to kingdom work?

Trying to answer these questions in the context of understanding God's call has led to three erroneous conclusions. Some believe God calls believers only to distinctly Christian vocations, such as being a pastor or teaching in a Christian school. Others take the opposite position that all vocational callings are the same, including the call to ministry leadership. Still others believe a person's vocation has nothing to do with God's call to Christian service (which is something you do at church *after* work). All of these conclusions are inadequate.

So, what is the relationship of God's universal call to Christian service and a believer's vocation? God calls every believer to Christian service. God's universal call to Christian service can be expressed through any honest vocation. God wants and needs Christian teachers, plumbers, attorneys, mechanics, nurses, and carpenters. There is, however, a distinct call to ministry leadership that often (though not always) results in employment in a ministry position.

God does not want every believer in a "Christian vocation" (defined as being compensated for ministry leadership), but every believer's work can and should be an avenue and venue for Christian service. God wants every believer to do his or her vocation in a Christian way. You may not teach in a Christian school, but you can still be a Christian schoolteacher. You may practice law in a secular firm, but you model sacred obedience to Jesus. God's universal call to Christian service must be lived through your vocation since it is such an important part of your life.

Sometimes believers feel so strongly about their profession or occupation that they express it in terms of being called. While this may seem confusing when using my definition of *call,* the wide range of meaning attached to the concept of call in Christian circles and popular culture makes this usage inevitable (and permissible). God certainly leads people to become veterinarians, dieticians, or truck drivers. These leadings are so profound that people sometimes refer to them as callings. Some are passionate about this sense of calling—and rightly so. God has made them for a unique purpose and role. Knowing you are in the center of God's plan for your life, particularly in the area of employment, is empowering!

On the other hand, some believers feel as if they are second-class spiritual citizens because they work in secular occupations while other believers serve in Christian vocations. This is, in plain terms, wrong! God wants *most* believers employed secularly, living the gospel among the people with whom they work. Any vocation, if legal and moral, can be a God-honoring occupation. A vital part of answering God's universal call to Christian service is serving God through your work—whatever that work may be.

The universal call to Christian service encompasses more than vocational choice. It is a call to serve God in every setting—including your hobbies, personal activities, and church responsibilities. Every believer is called to Christian service and is expected to consistently live the call in every area of life.

This universal call also relates to character development. You are called to sanctification—growth in holiness. You are called to live differently at work, at play, and at church. As a called-out one, you are supposed to live differently from the people around you. Answer God's universal call to Christian service and sanctification, and you will be on the way to fulfilling your responsibility as a disciple of Jesus.

A General Call to Ministry Leadership

While all believers have a universal call to Christian service, some believers also experience a general call to ministry leadership. Different people label this kind of experience differently. Various ways of describing this call include a call "to full-time Christian service," "to vocational Christian service," "to the gospel ministry," "to serve the Lord full time," or "to preach." All of these descriptions are helpful, but they also carry connotations that are sometimes colloquial, regional, and confusing.

The call to ministry leadership is not a call "to full-time Christian service" because all Christians are already called to full-time Christian service (remember the first part of this chapter). Every believer has a universal call to Christian service, so this second kind of call must be more than that. This call is also not a call "to vocational Christian service." Some people who have a call to ministry leadership are bivocational—intentionally choosing to provide part or all of their own financial support while they lead a ministry. Others are retired or self-salaried through other accumulated resources. Defining a call to ministry leadership in terms of payroll status is inadequate and misleading.

This kind of call is also not a call "to serve the Lord full time." Again, all believers serve the Lord full time. Neither is it a call "to the gospel ministry." Ministry leaders do, in a sense, serve the gospel; but, more specifically, ministry leaders serve God by doing things such as preaching, teaching, and sharing the gospel. This kind of call is also more than a call "to preach." Although preaching is essential in the church, it is not the role or responsibility of all ministry leaders. Defining this kind of call in terms of any particular ministerial or missional function is too confining.

Describing this kind of call in terms of "ministry leadership" removes much of this confusion. God specifically calls some men and women to leadership roles in his kingdom. They can be vocational or bivocational; full-time or part-time; and occupied with preaching, teaching, administrating, or any other ministerial or missional role. The key issue is *leadership*. All believers are called to *Christian service,* but God calls some believers to *ministry leadership*.

This kind of special call to ministry leadership is biblical. Some question this assertion, claiming that all believers are called alike and there is no special call to ministry leadership. This position seeks to diminish the differences between call experiences and reduce the concept of call to a generic, universal experience for all believers. Obviously, my understanding is based on a different model. One biblical example illustrates the uniqueness of the call to ministry leadership and how it differs from, and grows out of, the universal call to Christian service.

In Luke 5:1–11, Jesus met Peter and his partners after a long night of futile fishing. Jesus taught for a while and then told the tired fishermen to load their boats, sail to a certain place, and cast their nets. A miraculous catch resulted. Peter was overwhelmed and told Jesus, "Go away from me, because I'm a sinful man, Lord!" (v. 8). Jesus replied, "From now on you will be catching people" (v. 10). Luke then wrote this poignant conclusion: they "left everything, and followed Him" (v. 11).

The key point of this account that is related to call is Jesus asked Peter to leave fishing for ministry leadership. It was not enough for Peter to be a Christian fisherman. Jesus wants all fishermen to become Christians and wants most Christian fishermen to keep fishing. But not Peter! Jesus wanted Peter to leave fishing behind and make ministry leadership his complete focus.

Clearly, Jesus called Peter to a unique role. God still does this today. He calls some people to move beyond universal Christian service and answer his call to ministry leadership. God's call to ministry leadership is a general call, usually followed and clarified by a specific call to an assigned leadership role. That kind of call will be explained later in this chapter.

My general call to ministry leadership evolved slowly during my senior year of high school. In the summer before school started, my devotional Bible reading often had insights about being called into ministry and related themes. One night, several key verses seemed particularly significant as I considered my life and future. Still, my spiritual inexperience and desire to be sure delayed my commitment.

During that year, I thought, prayed, and talked with mentors and friends about my call. Fortunately, my pastor and others were very patient with me. They knew a call was an experience I had to be certain about. Although they worked with me, they never tried to convince me of my call. When I finally concluded that "God is calling me to ministry leadership," they were supportive.

My pastor did a good job of helping me understand my call. He helped me see that God's call was to ministry leadership but not yet a call to a particular kind of ministry or ministry assignment. He encouraged me to prepare for a nonministerial vocation in college to broaden my options for providing for myself while working in ministry leadership. He also encouraged me to try many different ministries as part of discovering God's particular call to a specific assignment. That call would come a few years later when I was called to be the pastor of my first church.

As a believer, you already have a universal call to Christian service. Like Peter, you may be called to devote yourself to ministry leadership. This second call emerges from the first. As you actively serve God, he opens your heart to further service and eventually to answering his call to lead others.

A general call to ministry leadership is a profound impression from God and a profound experience with God. Answering this call changes your priorities and establishes new directions and requirements for your life. Committing yourself to ministry leadership may require significant sacrifice. Like Peter, you may be called to leave "everything" (however God defines it in your life) and embark on a journey of faith unlike anything you previously imagined. Settling this issue and being sure of your call (as you will discover in a later chapter) are essential to effective kingdom leadership.

A Specific Call to a Ministry Assignment

For believers who have been called to ministry leadership, an additional call experience will happen at least once. After God calls a person to ministry leadership, he will later call him or her to a particular ministry assignment. For example, God may call you to ministry leadership in missions and later call you to a certain people group or mission field. God may call you to pastoral ministry leadership and later call you to a particular church as a pastor or an associate pastor. God may call you to teach, a general call to ministry leadership through educating others, and then call you to a certain school, college, or seminary.

Some assert that this kind of call does not happen, that ministry jobs are just jobs. You apply for them, take the best one you can find, and quit them when something better comes along. While this may be true for some support positions in ministry organizations, it is not true for leadership positions. A clear sense of call is necessary for anyone who assumes a ministry-leadership position in a church or Christian organization.

This kind of call is often easier to discern than the general call to ministry leadership because it involves another person or group actually offering you a position. This confirmation can give you greater confidence that God is calling. But be careful about this; just because someone offers you a leadership position does not mean God is calling you to take it. You must still sense God's call—a profound impression that establishes the specific parameters for your life related to the position.

For example, God may call you to collegiate ministry leadership. Later he will call you to a specific campus. The process for experiencing this aspect of God's call may be different, but the inner conviction must still come before you can confidently take the job. Listen to committees, supervisors, and board members as you discern the call, but be sure you listen mainly to God. His specific call to a ministry assignment is essential for effective, sustained Christian leadership.

One way to picture the process of God's calls is the following diagram. Your life is lived within the ever-narrowing parameters of God's calls—{his universal call to Christian service}, [his general call to ministry leadership], and (his specific call to a ministry assignment or position).

$$\left\{ \left[\left(\text{Your Life} \right) \right] \right\}$$

Again, all believers share a universal call to Christian service {the largest bracket}, some are called to ministry leadership [the next bracket], and those called to ministry leadership will be called to a specific assignment (the inner bracket).

Learn to live within the parameters of God's call for your life! Obedience to God's call is the safest, most satisfying life possible. As you experience his call, you will prove this to be true over and over again.

Three Ways God Calls

CHAPTER 3

Listening to ministry leaders tell their call stories might lead you to believe God calls people to ministry leadership or to a specific ministry assignment in an infinite number of ways. Every story is unique because God works with each person in a special way on an individual basis, creating a broad range of experiences with God. In the Bible God also called people in a variety of ways, often through unusual means, with each person having a unique experience with him.

Still, there are definite patterns to how God calls. Studying biblical call experiences reveals three primary patterns, or ways, God calls. You will be frustrated if you expect God to duplicate a particular biblical call experience to clarify your call. Those calls were unique to the persons involved. These biblical incidents are examples of God's call, not stories to be duplicated or copied. When you discover the patterns in biblical call experiences, you can better understand how God is working in your life.

As we consider the three ways God calls, it is easy to think that one is more spiritual or significant than the others. Don't make that mistake. When God calls, it is always a supernatural experience. God's calls are significant because of who is calling and what he is calling you to do. The circumstances of your call are not as important as the source and purpose of your call. Remember, no matter how God calls, it is always a supernatural experience.

God calls through *sudden experiences, reasoned decisions,* and the *prompting of others*. As each of these is described and illustrated, understand that they are broad descriptions of the ways God calls. They are not rigid categories. God's dynamic interactions with believers cannot be rigidly charted and itemized. Quantifying and qualifying biblical and contemporary call experiences, however, is helpful for creating shared categories for dialogue and understanding.

Although I will discuss the categories separately, many people have blended experiences. For example, a sudden experience with God might be followed by confirmation from fellow church members. A reasoned decision over time might culminate with a sudden experience with God. The prompting of others might initiate the call, only to have it finalized through careful deliberation. Again, God's calls are a dynamic process. The three categories help us understand God's call but do not put God in a box. God's ways can't be reduced to a formula.

Over years of teaching about call, I have informally surveyed students to discover which of these three ways is most common. Amazingly, seminary students report about an equal number of call experiences from each category. This confirms that all three are still valid ways of experiencing God's call. It also confirms that God still works in a variety of ways to call believers to ministry leadership and specific leadership assignments.

God Calls through Sudden Experiences

The first way God calls is through a sudden or dramatic experience. God called Moses to deliver Israel from Egypt by speaking from a burning bush (Exod. 3). The Lord called Saul (Paul) to ministry leadership through a blinding light on the road to Damascus (Acts 9). In both of these stories God spoke clearly while revealed in supernatural light. Each was an overwhelming, dramatic experience for the recipient. Each call was an unmistakable encounter with God.

Sometimes God calls like this. Often this kind of call comes during a life *crisis*. God intersects our lives powerfully, dramatically, and unmistakably. He speaks clearly, distinctly. A sudden or dramatic experience like this can be emotionally draining. It can also be frightening and cause us to wonder, *What just happened to me?* Some doubt that God still calls this way. Biblical examples, the stories of other leaders, and my experience have convinced me otherwise.

My call to leave pastoral ministry and become a denominational executive occurred during a sudden, dramatic encounter with God. When it happened, I was busy leading the church of my dreams. Five years before, our family had moved to Oregon to lead a small group starting a new church. We were as happy and fulfilled in ministry as we could imagine possible. Our church was growing, our family was happy, and life was very good.

Our life insurance provider sent me a letter offering an inexpensive expansion of our coverage. Because I had three small children at the time, it seemed like a good idea to take them up on their offer. The additional coverage required a routine medical exam. I made the appointment expecting to breeze through, get the insurance, and continue the terrific life we had.

God had another plan. My physician insisted on a full physical examination. To my surprise he found a lump on my thyroid. After several tests, the nature of the lump remained a mystery and it had to be removed. My surgeon assured me it was probably nothing to worry about in a young man my age. He took a cautious approach, removing the lump and sending me home to recover. Only in a worst-case scenario would the rest of my thyroid need to be removed with a second surgery.

Five days later, my surgeon called my home and said, "Jeff, have you eaten anything yet today?" My heart sank. There was only one reason to lead with that question—more surgery, and soon! My "nothing to worry about" lump was thyroid cancer. Later that evening I was in the hospital preparing for a second surgery. My remaining thyroid tissue had to be removed and, because of complications from the previous surgery, there was concern about preserving my ability to speak. Suddenly everything about our dream life was going terribly wrong.

Over the weeks all this was happening, the executive director search committee from the Northwest Baptist Convention contacted me and asked me to become a candidate, enter the interview process with them, and consider changing ministry assignments. This confused me. I was very happy being a pastor. I had never been interested in denominational leadership. Although I supported my denomination, my knowledge of how it worked was minimal. The committee process progressed over the same time frame as my health crisis unfolded.

It was a troubling time. Why was God allowing all this? What was his plan for me? How were these circumstances supposed to fit together? Were they related or just an unfortunate coincidence? All of this was swirling through my mind as I prepared for the second surgery.

My surgery was scheduled for late evening. After delivering me to the surgical area, my nurse said, "Your surgical team will be here in a little while. Until then, I'm going to let you rest quietly in this side room." He left me alone with my thoughts—and with God.

It had been a whirlwind day. After the morning call from my surgeon, we had to phone our families, tell our children, alert church leaders, cry a little, pack for the hospital, and cover as many details as possible to manage an uncertain future. There had not been much time to pray or be alone with God. So, taking advantage of the moment, I asked God a question.

One simple question—"Father, why is this happening to me?"—would change my life forever. Before I asked, I prayed, "Father, your answer to all our prayers about this situation has been no. We asked you to remove the lump. You didn't, and I had surgery. We asked you to keep it from being cancer. You didn't, and now I am having a second surgery. It is all so confusing. Father, why is this happening to me?"

The tone of the question is important. It was not a belligerent accusation, as if my cancer were unfair. It was not a faithless whine, like a spoiled child who thinks nothing bad should ever happen to him. My prayer was an honest question, a simple question, as I tried to understand why God was allowing these circumstances in my life.

What happened next is hard to explain. You may read this and rationalize it as a hallucination or an emotional experience. Telling this experience is risky on my part. However, defending its authenticity is unnecessary. What happened simply happened. My life was changed by the experience, and my ministry was completely redirected.

When I asked, "Father, why is this happening to me?" God's presence filled the room. His presence was tangible. I was terrified yet peaceful. It was a surreal moment. Then God spoke, clearly and precisely. It's hard to say if it was an audible voice or simply a verbal spiritual impression. Either way, God spoke definitively about my future: "Jeff, you belong to me. You don't belong to your family, your church, or your dream for your future. You belong to me. I will take you into and out of what I decide. You belong to me."

I then asked a second question: "Father, does this mean I am leaving pastoral ministry and going to the convention?" God answered, "You belong to me. Be ready for whatever I call you to do." And then, as suddenly as he appeared, God's presence left the room.

Over the next few minutes my thoughts were sharply focused. I knew I would be cured of cancer (and I have been). I knew I would not lose my voice. I knew I would leave the church. I knew I would become a denominational leader and leave pastoral ministry. I knew my understanding of my ministry future was changed forever. I knew God had called me to a new ministry assignment, really a new ministry lifestyle.

God called me through a sudden, dramatic encounter with him. As with Moses, Paul, and others in the Bible and church history, God revealed himself to me in a powerful and personal way. I was not seeking the experience. I don't ever expect it to be duplicated. I have a hard time adequately describing it. But I am sure of this: God met me that day. He called me in an unmistakable way.

Many times this kind of experience is glorified as the best kind of call. Several reminders and cautions will help you keep this type of experience in perspective. First, God calls in different ways, and all his ways are supernatural. Second, God wants us to seek and worship him, not seek or worship an experience with him. Be careful not to glorify an experience with God more than God himself. Third, these kinds of experiences usually surprise people when they happen. I was not seeking or expecting this kind of experience. Neither have I sought one since, nor will I in the future. God reveals himself in unique ways to accomplish his purpose, not to titillate our spiritual senses or give us something to brag about. Finally, this kind of experience is rare. Even in the Bible, God did not communicate this way with Moses and Paul every time he called them to do something. So it is with us. God may call you through a sudden, dramatic spiritual encounter, but that does not normalize the process for every future call experience.

God Calls through Reasoned Decisions

A second way God calls is through a reasoned decision or cognitive process. As with a sudden experience, this kind of call has biblical precedent. Paul, the same person who had the sudden experience on the Damascus road, also heard God's call through other means. On one missionary journey his mission team "went through the region of Phrygia and Galatia and were prevented by the Holy Spirit from speaking the message in the province of Asia. When they came to Mysia, they tried to go into Bithynia, but the Spirit of Jesus did not allow them. So, bypassing Mysia, they came down to Troas" (Acts 16:6–8).

During a night in Troas, Paul had a dream in which a Macedonian man asked him to "cross over . . . and help us" (Acts 16:9). The team then "made efforts to set out for Macedonia" (Acts 16:10). A common misunderstanding of this incident is that Paul had a dream, and instantly the team was in Macedonia preaching to the man. Not so!

First, the team spent weeks wandering through several provinces trying to discover God's direction. They walked and walked and walked while looking for an opening for the gospel or a place to plant a church. None materialized. Second, even after Paul had the dream, the team still had to arrange travel to Macedonia. More process! Finally, and somewhat humorously, when the team arrived in Macedonia, the man turned out to be a woman, Lydia.

The team concluded "that God had called" (Acts 16:10) them to evangelize in Macedonia after months of travel, trying other alternatives, a dream, and more travel. Paul, the same man who was called dramatically on the Damascus road, worked with his team through a reasoned process to discover God's call to Macedonia.

My call to plant a church in Oregon came through a reasoned decision. During doctoral studies focused on missions and evangelism, the compelling need for church planting in major cities became a burden. The need in cities in the western United States was particularly intriguing to me. Over time, I became convinced that I was called to start a culture-current church in a major western city.

How did this happen? It happened over time—after deliberative *contemplation* and many discussions with my professors, friends, wife, and mentors. It was not an easy process. Taking the risk to move our family to a new place, start a church with just a few people, and manage the financial issues was challenging. Fear was a factor. What if the new church failed, we suffered financially, or (it's hard to admit this part) my reputation were harmed?

Once the decision to plant a church was made, the next question was "Where?" Again, a reasoned process ensued. I contacted a mission board. I worked with friends and acquaintances responsible for church planting. For a long time we assumed we would move to Arizona. Why? Again, a reasoned decision. My wife and I had grown up in a similar climate. We thought, *We like hot, dry weather. Let's go to Phoenix.*

Eventually, I met a man who recruited church planters for Oregon. At first we were not interested. After all,

Portland, Oregon, is not hot or dry! But eventually every other door closed. We were left with one viable option—starting a church in a suburb of Portland. We concluded, like Paul's missionary team when all other options closed, that God had called us to Oregon.

Throughout this process we were praying and seeking assurance of God's call. We wanted a clear confirmation that we were doing the right thing. We kept thinking it would come in an insightful moment of Bible reading, through an intense conviction during a worship service, or through some dramatic encounter with God. But none of that happened.

We simply walked forward, processing the information God was allowing us to learn and discerning his leading through the circumstances he allowed. We kept moving forward through open doors and being redirected by doors that closed. Looking back, we now see God's direction more clearly than when we were living through the process. At the time, we wondered whether our reasoned decision was an authentic call experience. Hindsight, spiritual maturity, further biblical insight into the concept of call, and God's blessing on our ministry in Oregon have convinced us of the validity of experiencing God's call through a reasoned process.

God sometimes calls through reasoned decisions, through the unfolding process of circumstances he allows. This type of call is supernatural. God is overseeing the process. Spiritual discernment reveals God's hand behind the process and his intentional, methodical revelation through this kind of call.

God Calls through the Prompting of Others

The third way God calls is through the prompting of others. God sometimes sends a messenger, as when Samuel selected David to be the future king of Israel (1 Sam. 16). Other times, God speaks through the church (or the larger Christian community) to reveal his will. One example of this was the initiation of the missionary movement through the church at Antioch. During a worship service, the Holy Spirit said, "Set apart for Me Barnabas and Saul [Paul] for the work that I have called them to" (Acts 13:2).

Paul and Barnabas were participating in the worship service. The obvious question is, "Why didn't the Holy Spirit just speak directly to these men?" Instead, the Spirit prompted church members to communicate the call to the mission team. They told Paul and Barnabas about God's plan and commissioned them for service. The call to missions came through the prompting of others.

For many years I had heard others report this kind of experience, but nothing like this had ever happened to me. I had never had a call that came through the prompting of others. My call to Golden Gate Seminary changed this.

About two years before the presidential search process began, a good friend and ministry peer talked with me one day. He said, "Jeff, God is going to call you to be the president of Golden Gate Seminary. You need to begin preparing yourself." I tried to laugh it off, but he insisted I take him seriously. The whole conversation was surprising and puzzling. I tried to forget about it.

A few months later another friend said, "I need to tell you something. God wants you to prepare yourself to be the president of Golden Gate Seminary." Again I tried to laugh it off. And once again, the messenger insisted I take him seriously.

Over the two years prior to the official start of the search process, many different people delivered a similar message to me. In every case I asked the person, "Have you talked with anyone else about this?" Each one assured me they had not. It seemed God was speaking to a significant number of my ministry friends, peers, and colleagues and prompting them to deliver the same message to me.

My wife and I agreed we would listen for God's call through the church—in the form of our ministry peers and the seminary trustees. We knew the trustees were ultimately responsible for discerning God's will about selecting the president. Golden Gate also used an advisory council to give input into the process. We prayed for God to give the advisory council and trustees unusual unity about me if I was to be president. Ultimately, that is what happened, confirming the personal messages we had heard throughout the previous two years.

My call to the seminary was not a sudden, dramatic spiritual encounter. Neither was it a reasoned decision (no reasonable person would want the job!). God called me through the prompting of others. He sent messengers to shape my thinking toward the position, and then the advisors and trustees confirmed the decision. When offered the position, we were ready to respond. We had already concluded we would trust the discernment of the Christian *community* over our own judgment.

God called me through the prompting of others. My call to Golden Gate is as sure as the dramatic experience that called me to the convention or the reasoned process that called me to church planting.

God's calls are sure and secure no matter which of these ways he uses to communicate them to us. Be open to God's calling you through sudden experiences, reasoned decisions, or the prompting of others. Your call may come through a *crisis,* through *contemplation,* or through the *community.* God has different ways of calling in different circumstances and seasons of life. And, as previously mentioned, sometimes these experiences overlap or complement one another. However God calls you, listen carefully and say yes!

Who God Calls

CHAPTER 4

Many people struggle with hearing or obeying God's call because they simply do not believe they are worthy of being called. Some potential ministry leaders struggle with poor spiritual self-esteem, a nagging sense of inadequacy, shame for past sins, or a lack of confidence in their usefulness to God. If you are struggling with any of these issues, take heart! Many other believers are struggling as well—including ministry leaders. Most leaders have a strong sense of personal frailty and moral weakness. We know ourselves and wonder, honestly, how or why God would ever want to use people like us.

But he does! God calls people like you and me to serve him as ministry leaders. He calls real people, with real limitations, and confounds all of us by using us to do his work. He calls people who have baggage from their past. He calls those who never expected it. He calls people others would have never chosen. He calls according to his purpose and plan. God calls people with a vision of who they can become and empowers them to do more than they ever imagined.

One good example of this is the people God called and used to bring Jesus into the world. The New Testament opens with a genealogy, a listing of the people in the family tree of Jesus on Joseph's side of the family (Matt. 1:1–17). Most people would choose the best and brightest, most hopeful and holiest to create the lineage of Jesus. God chose otherwise.

God Calls Unexpected People

God included "Judah and his brothers" (v. 2) in the lineage of Jesus. The inclusion of Judah—not Reuben, the firstborn brother—is noteworthy. There were actually three brothers older than Judah, all passed over in favor of Judah in the lineage of Jesus. David, a son of Jesse, is also included in the list. He is another example of a younger brother who was chosen over his siblings. In David's case, he had seven older brothers who were considered but passed over. David was chosen not only to be king but also to be in the royal lineage of Jesus.

Israelite culture valued firstborn sons and preserved both family and community through them. For example, a family's legal residence and identity were maintained through the firstborn son. Property remained in families through transfer rights from firstborn son to firstborn son. The royal and priestly offices were also passed down this same way. Oldest sons had special responsibilities to protect, defend, and extend a family's influence.

Given these cultural and legal mandates, it is even more surprising that Judah and David were chosen. Remember, human ability and natural charisma did not usually trump the legal expectations of firstborn sons— these practices were preserved without reference to the firstborn's leadership ability. God did not choose Judah and David randomly but to make a clear point. God established the lineage of Jesus by his grace and according to his purpose, which superseded all legal requirements.

God chose some unexpected people to bring Jesus into the world. God specializes in using people no one expects. Consider these other biblical examples. Peter was a commercial fisherman and Paul a religious terrorist. God used these men to transform the early Christian movement from a scattered band of frightened disciples to a missionary force changing an empire. God chose a physician, Luke, to write a huge portion of the New Testament. He changed John from being a position-craving follower to the humble disciple who wrote about God's love and our need to love one another. In the Old Testament, God used Gideon to lead an army, Deborah to judge a nation, and Ruth to bear a son (Jesse, the father of David). All of these people—by their backgrounds and circumstances—were unexpected choices, people unlikely to make a significant contribution to God's work.

Younger leaders who are still considering or processing God's call often look at more experienced leaders and assume they have always been as committed and effective as they are now. That is not the case. Recently, while speaking on calling, I projected my picture at the age when I was called to ministry leadership. What a goofy kid—big black glasses, slicked-down hair, pimples, and a multicolored shirt that (I thought!) would attract girls. Seeing that young man reminded my audience (and me) that God calls unexpected, unpolished people to serve him. God calls people for who they can become by his grace, not for who they already are.

We sometimes assume a God-called leader is born with a spiritual silver spoon in his or her mouth. Some ministry leaders were reared in Christian homes with many spiritual advantages. Thank God for that blessing. But many are also from more difficult spiritual backgrounds. My background was more like the latter. Considering my lack of spiritual heritage, no one would have predicted my becoming a seminary president. My call demonstrates God's grace. He calls unexpected people to serve him.

God Calls Immoral People

Three women mentioned in Jesus' lineage—Tamar, Rahab, and Bathsheba—had dubious moral reputations. Tamar was Judah's daughter-in-law (Gen. 38). She posed as a cult prostitute and duped Judah into impregnating her. Rahab was a prostitute in Jericho who sided with the Israelites and helped deliver the city into their hands (Josh. 2). Bathsheba, referred to as Uriah's wife in the genealogy, was David's mistress. She committed adultery and was complicit in the murder of her husband (2 Sam. 11).

David is also listed in the lineage of Jesus. He is an enigma. He was "a man after [God's] own heart" (Acts 13:22) who was also an adulterous murderer, yet God included him in Jesus' family tree. Tamar, Rahab, Bathsheba, and David were all guilty of immoral acts still shocking even in our sex-saturated society.

God chooses and uses people who have sexual sin in their past. Many young adults do not answer God's call because they are racked with guilt over past sexual sin. They wonder how God could use someone who has violated God's standards for sexual behavior. Others have been victims of sexual abuse. They feel incredible guilt and misplaced responsibility for what happened to them. They wonder how God could use them when they have such a horrible secret from their past. Still others are victims of sex crimes, such as rape or assault. They, too, wonder why

God would call them after allowing such terrible events in their lives.

Sexual sin in your past does not disqualify you from future ministry leadership. God will forgive your sins. He will restore you if you were victimized. He cleanses you and makes you useful for his service. If God is calling you, don't use your sexual past as an excuse to disobey. Disobedience to God's call will have worse ramifications for your future than any sin—sexual or otherwise— in your past.

One friend with an immoral past did not become a Christian until he was twenty-one, which allowed for many years of licentious behavior as a teenager and young adult. His conversion delivered him from compulsive immorality, and soon after, God called him to ministry leadership. He struggled for years with guilt from his past. Yet, despite residual struggles with spiritual self-condemnation, he has persevered to overcome his past and use it as a platform for encouraging others to live morally pure lives.

Another friend was an incest victim. She has put that behind her and moved forward to become an effective missionary. God called another friend who had experimented with a homosexual lifestyle to ministry leadership among young adults. With so much sexual sin in our world, many (if not most) young adults simply do not reach adulthood without some moral issues to resolve. Yet they can be resolved, and God can use a restored person as a leader in his kingdom.

If a person was introduced to pornography in grade school, secretly viewed explicit videos his parents brought home, searched for popularity through sexual favors in high school, or lived with his girlfriend while in college, there is a sexual past to overcome. Some who were incest victims or who were date raped, fondled, abused, or misused sexually have sexual issues to overcome in answering God's call. However, none of these choices made or abuses endured make a person ineligible for God's call.

Still, be clear about this: once God calls you, he requires you to uphold the high standard of moral purity expected of ministry leaders. God calls people who have sexual sin or abuse *in their past*. God-called ministry leaders are held to a higher standard than other believers. Sure, sin is the same for all people, but the consequences of sexual sin in a ministry leader's life are far more devastating than the same failure by a follower. When a leader fails morally, trust is lost, community is fractured, relationships are broken, and children and young adults who look to us for moral guidance and inspiration are discouraged. These are serious consequences to be avoided at all costs.

If you have immorality in your past, God can still use you. If you have been victimized by another person's immoral choices, God can still use you. Listen for his call, and do not use your past as an excuse to ignore God and miss the future he has for you.

God Calls Anonymous People

Not everyone God calls to serve him will be a prominent, well-known leader. In fact, most ministry leaders serve in relative anonymity, known only to the people in their immediate circle of influence. Several people on Jesus' family tree—such as Perez, Hezron, Ram, Salmon, and Obed—are relatively unknown, except for God including them in Jesus' lineage.

The Bible also lists people without revealing or recording any details about their ministries. When Jesus called the Twelve, he included James, the son of Alphaeus, and Judas, the son of James. Jesus prayed all night prior to selecting these men. They served him faithfully and were still present when the early church organized and launched its ministry. Church tradition has sketchy information about their continued service, but they were apparently faithful to their calls until their deaths. Still, they served as relatively unknown leaders compared to Peter, James, and John. Sometimes, Jesus puts people on his team who will fill a role and work behind the scenes. Not everyone is a platform leader, public speaker, or executive leader.

When my children were younger, I coached many of their sports teams. One question I often asked the players in any sport was "What is the most important position on the field?" The correct answer, they learned, is "The position I'm playing!" If you don't think that's true, try playing a baseball game without a left fielder or a football game without a right guard. When God puts you on his team, he will give you a position to play. Play it! Don't worry about how insignificant it seems. Do your part in God's kingdom.

Other people in the Bible did remarkable things but are not even named. When early church leaders scattered because of the persecution of Stephen, they preached the gospel to Jews wherever they went. Some made it to Antioch, and "some of them, Cypriot and Cyrenian men . . . began speaking to the Hellenists, proclaiming the good news about the Lord Jesus" (Acts 11:19–20). When I get to heaven, I want to meet those men!

Why? Because those anonymous men took the risk to preach the gospel to the Gentiles. Without that breakthrough, the church at Antioch would not have formed. Without that church, the missionary movement would not have been launched. Without that movement, most people reading this book never would have had the opportunity to follow Jesus. Those anonymous men from Cyprus and Cyrene are heroes of the faith.

God calls some people who are relatively unknown and others who are completely unknown, but these people make significant contributions to God's work. God may be calling you, and you are resisting because you doubt your ability to maintain a prominent ministry. Or, you may think that what God is calling you to do is not very significant; therefore, it can't really be God calling! God calls people to various roles and assignments. Obey God and allow him to determine the scope and significance of what he assigns you to do.

God Calls Inconsistent People

Two men in Jesus' lineage were woefully inconsistent, yet they are considered two of the greatest leaders of all time. First, consider Abraham. He is an incredibly important figure through whom God inaugurated his covenant relationship with Israel. He is, by all measure, the father of our faith, yet he also passed his wife off as his sister on two occasions to avoid conflict and save his own skin. And what about David? He is called "a man after [God's] own heart" (Acts 13:22), but he also took Bathsheba as his mistress and arranged the killing of her husband.

What can you learn from God including such men in his plans? God uses people who are inconsistent. Some people are afraid to answer God's call because they know they won't always live up to his expectations. The simple truth is, you won't always live up to your call. You will make mistakes, disappoint God and others, and have days when you wonder why God ever called you in the first place. Don't despair! God calls you for the potential you have, not the perfection you demonstrate. Your usefulness to God is based on his consistency, not yours. Your call is sustained by God's faithfulness, not yours.

On my twenty-fifth anniversary in ministry leadership, I wrote a list of insights and conclusions I had learned. One of them was "I thought I would be a better man by now." When I started in ministry leadership, I assumed I would make amazing progress in Bible study, prayer, Scripture memory, preaching ability, and pastoral skills. I thought I would conquer my anger, master personal relationships, and learn to love everyone. I was wrong. My inconsistency in these areas makes me wonder why God continues to use me. You will have a similar experience. God-called ministry leaders grow in grace but never reach perfection. God delights in showing his strength through our weaknesses. Weakness, no matter how much we grow in God's grace, is an ever-present reality for ministry leaders—and it will be for you too.

God calls all kinds of people to serve him. Don't ignore God's call because you don't think you are the type of person God can use. Don't disqualify yourself because of past sin. Realize that God calls all kinds of people to a variety of roles, including some very obscure but important assignments that matter a great deal to him. Accept your frailty. God does. Accept your role no matter how insignificant it seems to you. God will use you despite your weaknesses, inadequacies, and inconsistencies.

So, don't make excuses based on your past or perceived inadequacies. Obey God's call in your life—whoever you are and wherever he assigns you.

Discerning God's Call

CHAPTER 5

How do you really *know* you are called to ministry leadership or to a specific ministry assignment? God calls through dramatic experiences, reasoned decisions, and the prompting of others. God calls through a crisis, through contemplation, and through community. That sounds so organized, so definitive. But often, God's call is a combination of these experiences. In hindsight they often seem very clear, but when you are in the middle of discovering God's call, things are not always so neatly ordered. Life is dynamic. God works in different ways with circumstances unique to each person. Our understanding is often murky, not always crystal clear. Discernment is required to really *know* God is calling.

You are in a relationship with God, an ever-changing process of learning from him, understanding his ways, and discovering more and more about him. This means a call process can be confusing. You struggle to be sure you are hearing from God because you know the life-altering consequences of your decision. This is one issue we all really need to get right.

There is, fortunately, some evidence that God is calling you that can help you sort out this process. This is not forensic evidence. You can't check your spiritual DNA and know God's call. This kind of evidence is the collected experience and wisdom of many who have clarified God's call. Talking with dozens of ministry leaders about their call experiences reveals certain common denominators often present among the called. These commonalities are helpful when discerning either a call to ministry leadership or a call to a specific ministry assignment. These characteristics of call experiences are signposts to help you find your way to a final conclusion in answer to the essential question "Is God calling me?"

Inner Peace

We have already emphasized the definition of *call* as a "profound impression from God." This is an inner work of the Spirit touching you deeply. A call is an experience with God, an inner experience difficult to quantify. In plain terms, you simply know it in your heart.

The importance of inner peace or inner conviction about your call can't be underestimated. When God calls, you will come to a core conviction that you have heard him speak and that you must obey. You will then be able to move steadfastly forward, buffered against opposition and turmoil resisting your call, with quiet confidence that God is leading you. The peace of God "which surpasses every thought, will guard your hearts and your minds in Christ Jesus" (Phil. 4:7). An inner conviction about your call can give you strength to endure anything—from verbal abuse to financial struggles and even including martyrdom.

Michael Sattler, an early martyr, is a remarkable example of this. You can read about him in *The Anabaptist Story* by William Estep.[1] It was said of him, "Seemingly nothing could destroy [his] calm self-composure. Even the sentence [torture and death] . . . failed to shake him." His call secured him as he faced incredible pain and eventual death.

His martyrdom is described this way: "The torture, a prelude to the execution, began at the marketplace, where a piece was cut from Sattler's tongue. Pieces of flesh were torn from his body with red hot tongs. He was forged to a cart. . . . The tongs were applied five times. . . . After being bound to a ladder with ropes and pushed into a fire . . . the unshakeable Sattler prayed for his persecutors. . . . As soon as the ropes on his wrist were burned, Sattler raised two fingers . . . giving the promised signal to the brethren that a martyr's death was bearable."

1. William Estep, *The Anabaptist Story* (Grand Rapids: Eerdmans, 1996), 71.

What enables a person to endure such pain and torture? What sustains Christian martyrs today? The answer: a convincing, compelling inner sense of destiny. In other words, a clear call from God. Nothing else will sustain you through the ups and downs of ministry, much less such brutal suffering for the sake of the gospel. Ministry leaders, now and in the future, will need this kind of confidence in God's call to endure ever-increasing opposition to the gospel.

Part of having this inner peace is developing security in Jesus Christ. When you were saved, you were made eternally secure. You don't become eternally secure when you die—you are as secure today, in Christ, as you will ever be. One evidence that God is calling you is a deep, settled, inner conviction about the call. God will give you unexplainable, indescribable peace as you hear from him and obey his will for your life.

Confirmation by Others

Because one way God calls is through the prompting of others, it might seem like needless repetition to include this as an evidence of God's call. God calls through the prompting of others, but he often confirms his call, no matter how it comes, through other people.

Sometimes this can be a direct message, as when people came to me about my call to Golden Gate. Most of the time, however, this confirmation takes other forms.

Sometimes it is informal confirmation. For example, a friend or church member will compliment your effectiveness in ministry and ask whether you have ever considered that God might be calling you to ministry leadership. Or, perhaps you go on a mission trip and do an exceptional job relating to people of a different culture. As a result, the host missionary challenges you to consider a call to missions. These informal comments are often the way God first gets our attention about considering his call.

Other times this can be a more formal process. Seminaries and mission boards require extensive references for candidates who apply for admission or appointment. One reason for this is to gauge the validity of a person's call by asking others for their perspective on it. After all, why would a church send someone to seminary or the mission field if members had not observed some evidence of God's call in that person's life?

Discovering God's call, however, is not a popularity contest or a public-opinion poll. So, whose opinion should you consider, and whose counsel should you heed when considering whether God is calling you? Several groups of people come to mind.

First, consider the input of spiritual leaders. Your pastor, collegiate minister, youth minister, Sunday school teacher, or Bible study leader can be a barometer indicating your call. If any of these people have serious reservations about your being called, you should listen carefully. These spiritual guides know you well, have experience in ministry to gauge your suitability, and want the best for you. If they raise a red flag, pay heed. On the other hand, if any of these urge you to consider that God might be calling you to ministry leadership, you should also pay attention. Spiritual leaders who know you well are important sources of confirmation of your call.

Second, listen to your family. This can be tricky. Some God-called younger leaders come from non-Christian families. It might seem as if you should ignore their opinion. Not always. Discernment is required to know how to interpret their input. Some non-Christian families want their children to avoid ministry leadership because it convicts them of their sin, prevents materialistic goals from being achieved, or is otherwise disappointing. If these are the reasons, reject your family's counsel and answer God's call.

On the other hand, some non-Christian family members have insight into your character and personality. Intuitively, based on their observation of ministry leaders, they know you are entering ministry for the wrong reasons or with a character flaw that will undermine your effectiveness. One friend told me, "My dad was not a believer. He resisted paying for me to go to college to enter the ministry because he thought I was lazy. He told me, 'You will never make it in the ministry, and I won't support that decision.' It was tough to admit he was right. So I got a job and started putting myself through school.

My dad later changed his mind and told me, 'Now that you know how to work, you can make it in the ministry. It's a hard job, but I will help you get trained.'"

My friend was surprised that his father knew enough about the ministry to consider it "a hard job." In this case, his father's opposition was not to the ministry but was based on his knowledge of his son's character flaw—laziness, which no minister can afford. Listening to his father's reluctance about his call enabled my friend to correct a character flaw on the way to answering his call to pastoral ministry (and earning his father's respect).

Sadly, listening to your family can also be unsettling even when they are believers. Some Christian families want "the best" for their children but interpret it to mean money, position, and keeping the grandchildren close by. God has another agenda—his kingdom's advance. When a family, even a Christian family, opposes your call, you must obey God.

Third, if you are married, you should listen to your spouse. Ministry leadership is a team effort. When God calls a person who is already married, the spouse must be included in the decision. Even when only the called person will be in ministry leadership, a commitment from both partners is still required. Sometimes this means working together and sharing the same call. Missionary couples often have a joint calling. Other times, however, it means spousal support of a shared calling. For example, one effective pastor is married to a legal secretary. His wife is very committed to her career yet is also totally supportive of her husband's ministry. Spousal support does not mean you must share the same occupation, but it does mean your spouse will support you and cooperate as you pursue your call.

Effectiveness in Ministry

Another way to discover whether God is calling you is to evaluate your effectiveness in ministry. Younger people may not have much experience to measure, but they can still analyze and consider the results they have achieved. More mature believers, perhaps persons considering God's call after many years in secular employment but active church participation, have a longer track record to ponder.

Effectiveness in ministry does not mean stellar success in everything you have attempted. It means you have seen God work through you, appropriate to your skill level and opportunity, to effect spiritual results in people's lives. For example, when you teach a Bible lesson, do your students readily grasp spiritual truth? When you visit a sick person, are you complimented on your bedside manner? When you witness to a lost person, is it easy to present the gospel and ask for a commitment? When you preach, do you seem to be carried along by God accomplishing more than you ever imagined?

These are the kinds of questions to ask as you analyze your effectiveness. Another measure is the opportunities God and others give you for ministry leadership. Are you someone people often ask to lead in prayer, lead a Bible study, lead a decision-making process at church, or lead short-term mission teams? Leaders have followers, and if people often indicate they want you to lead, then perhaps God is calling you to ministry leadership.

Another consideration is spiritual results. Ministry leadership is more than using your gifts for God. Ministry leadership is a mysterious combination of God using your gifts to do more than you ever could have done on your own. Ministry leaders often marvel at the results God accomplishes—people saved, lives transformed, mourners encouraged, sick people healed. All of this happens through us. We marvel at how God uses his called leaders. One way to know God is calling you into ministry leadership is the fact that he is already doing some amazing things through you. You see God at work through you, perhaps in small ways, and sense he wants to do much more as you devote yourself entirely to ministry leadership.

Joy in the Ministry

God-called leaders have bad days, but for the most part, ministry leadership is a joy for them. They enjoy a deep sense of fulfillment as God works through them. They like people and enjoy being part of developing them into the image of Jesus. God-called ministry leaders find joy in the ministry.

God gives each of us desires or passions for certain activities, involvements, or commitments. God's call is often found at the intersection of our passion and the opportunities he allows. When ministry is your passion, it may be an indication God is calling you to ministry leadership. If you can't imagine a more fulfilling life than one devoted to leading people in ministry, God may be calling you.

A particular issue in this area is the joy (or lack of it) in working with people. As ministry leaders sometimes say on bad days, "The ministry would be great if it weren't for the people." Working with people, all kinds of people, is the most difficult part of ministry leadership. Yet those same people (and sometimes the exact same exasperating people) can be a source of your greatest joy.

Analyzing how you feel about working with people is an important part of considering your call. My oldest son, who played small-college football, once served a church internship to investigate whether he was being called into ministry leadership. After six months he said, "Dad, I just have one question for you about the ministry. How do you put up with all the whining? I mean, really. Don't you want to tell church people to just grow up?

Most of these people wouldn't last five minutes on our football team."

My son was not being called into ministry! He was getting very little joy from the church people he was serving. Most ministry leaders know that some people whine and need to grow up, but most of us ignore the childish people and focus our attention on the larger number of people who are growing, serving, and learning under our direction. Today my son is happily serving the Lord and his church through a secular vocation and volunteer ministry. Part of knowing he was not called to ministry leadership was the limited amount of joy he received from dealing with church people during his internship.

Ministry is draining. People can be extremely difficult, but ministry is a people business. Finding joy in the ministry is about finding satisfaction in working with people. Joy comes from watching people be saved and grow into mature believers. Ministry leadership involves celebrating weddings, anniversaries, graduations, and memorial services. It's baptisms, mission trips, church socials, and ministry projects. Living, loving, laughing, as well as managing difficult relationships, are all part of working with God's people. If that brings you joy and fuels your passion, if you cannot imagine anything more fulfilling, then perhaps God is calling you to ministry leadership.

Realistic Expectations about the Ministry

God-called people enter the ministry for the right reason and with reasonable expectations. Confusion on either point leads to frustration as ministry leaders struggle in a role they were not made for or expect fulfillment of personal needs that never comes. If you want to be in ministry leadership, be sure your desire is in response to God's call and not to satisfy your unrealistic expectations about the ministry.

Some people enter ministry looking for personal fulfillment or to satisfy the expectations of others. Ministry leaders sometimes pursue promotions and larger ministry opportunities expecting to find fulfillment through personal recognition or financial gain. Those who enter ministry to please parents or grandparents, or to meet the expectations of mentors or other spiritual guides, end up frustrated. You simply can't base your call on pleasing others or satisfying interpersonal needs. It must be in response to God alone.

Some people enter ministry for the right reasons but with unrealistic expectations of what ministry will do for them. Ministry is not a means to personal fulfillment. It does not automatically solve issues like poor self-esteem, poor self-discipline, or other character deficiencies. One person told me, "I thought getting into the ministry would solve my moral struggles." Another claimed, "The ministry was my ticket to feeling good about myself." One church sent a prospective student to seminary "so you can straighten him out." These kinds of character issues are never resolved by entering ministry (or ministry training) but must be resolved before you will be sustained or fulfilled in ministry.

From the outside it's also easy to have wrong expectations about what ministry leadership will be like. You might make a short-term mission trip and think you understand what a lifetime of international mission service will involve. Then when you arrive on the field full-time, you discover it is very different from what you expected. Or perhaps you listen to your pastor preach and wonder, *How hard can it be?* Then when the weekly grind of preaching becomes part of your work, you are overwhelmed with the demand.

Be sure you enter ministry leadership or change to a different ministry assignment for the right reason. The only valid reason is God's call. If God calls you to ministry leadership, answer his call. If God calls you to a new ministry assignment, take it. But be sure you make these decisions in response to God's call. Avoid the trap of entering ministry to meet your personal needs or of having unrealistic expectations of what ministry will be like.

These signposts require discernment to realize how they relate to discovering or understanding your call. God shapes our understanding of his call by giving inner peace.

He allows encouragement and confirmation from people who know us well and want the best for us. Effectiveness and joy in the ministry may indicate a growing sense of call. As God shapes your understanding of his call, be sure you are listening for God's voice alone. Be sure you are not entering ministry to meet personal needs. Avoid unrealistic expectations of what ministry will be like. Discern how God is working to reveal his call—or not—and respond in obedience to him.

The Effects of God's Call

CHAPTER 6

G od's call has personal implications and tangible effects on your view of life and ministry. In short, it uniquely impacts your relationship with God and others by changing your perspective and empowerment for ministry. Assurance of his call gives you confidence, helps you persevere through tough times, gives you appropriate authority to lead, and is a source of humility. Each of these effects of God's call has ramifications for your role and outlook as a leader.

But God gives all believers confidence, perseverance, authority, and humility. So why are these singled out as unique effects of God's call? These qualities are not exclusive to leaders, but as a leader, you will need them in extra measure, and God will give them in greater dimension. God's call creates the need for additional confidence, perseverance, authority, and humility while at the same time opening the door for further development of these qualities through the challenges leaders face. As always, where God allows or creates need, he also supplies. Leaders need an extra dose of these qualities. God's call is one means to develop these resources.

God's Call Gives You Confidence

When God calls you to ministry leadership or to a specific leadership assignment, you can have confidence in your ability and suitability for the job. Most leaders face daunting responsibilities and wonder whether they are up to the task. In our own strength and initiative, the answer is clearly no. But something mysterious and powerful happens when God calls. His call gives us confidence to do what we have been called to do.

God's call gives confidence because he calls us to join him in his work. God is with us all the time while we are doing his work. Leaders especially need to remember this. Chuck Swindoll wrote a little booklet called "The Lonely Whine of the Top Dog" describing the isolation and ensuing loneliness of leaders. Leaders are often lonely. We work with confidential information, on projects that require circumspection, and with people on private matters. We also spend time alone studying and preparing for public ministry. Leaders, especially pastors of small churches or missionaries in isolated locations, often have no peers or partners who share their work. All of these factors contribute to a sense of isolation and loneliness.

But God is with you! He is always with you. Jesus promised his continued presence in believers through the Holy Spirit, and leaders throughout church history testify of experiencing God's presence in critical moments. The source of our confidence as leaders is God with us. Once, when my oldest son was about four, we were walking through a dark church building trying to find a light switch. Suddenly his little hand reached out and grabbed mine. I jumped about a foot! Then he said, "It's OK, Dad, I'm with you." When you are scared, it's good to have someone with you. One of my favorite prayers as I walk into a meeting or onto a platform to speak is "Lord, here we go." This simple prayer reinforces that ministry leadership is more "we" than "me." God is always with us.

You can also have confidence in God's call because your abilities are suitable for the job he assigns. Most leaders are aware of their inadequacies. They can list their weaknesses, particularly in light of the perceived strengths needed for a particular ministry position. Instead of focusing on your shortcomings, focus on your strengths and the contribution you can make by answering God's call. For example, one pastor was a superb preacher and motivator. When he left his church, the pastor who followed him was better at organizing and leading through others. The second pastor was confident in his abilities and decided to focus on his strengths rather than wallow in pointless comparison to the previous pastor's strengths. The church prospered under this shift in leadership skill sets. To become a more healthy church, this different leadership style was required in that season of the church's life.

Ministry organizations and churches need certain types of leaders during different seasons. No leader is strong in all areas. All leaders have a unique set of strengths, abilities, or talents to contribute. Your focus must be on doing what you can with the talents you have for the time you are called to lead in any setting. Do not be immobilized by focusing on your weaknesses, on what you are not able to do. Focus on who you are and what you are able to do. When you lead, do what you *can* do. In other words, "Give 'em what you've got."

God knows who you are and what you can contribute when he calls you. He assigns you to an appropriate ministry setting for the season your contribution will be helpful. When your church, mission, ministry, or school needs another kind of leader, God will call you away and put someone else in your place. In the meantime, assume God has you in your current place (or will call you to the right place) and get busy making your unique contribution to the kingdom. Play to your strengths!

God's Call Aids in Perseverance

A pastor of a church for more than thirty years told me the secret of his longevity. "Well," he mused, "discouragement and a pastor search committee never showed up on the same day." Most ministry leaders have Black Mondays . . . or Tuesdays . . . or Wednesdays. . . . Ministry leaders, like everyone else, get discouraged. Discouragement leads to depression. Depression means lost hope. Lost hope means we give up and eventually quit.

God's call helps us stay in the game. Why? Because we realize we have been placed in our role by someone we do not want to disappoint or disregard. People blessed with godly parents often make behavioral choices based on honoring their parents. One person told me, "There were some things in high school I simply wouldn't do because I didn't want to disappoint my mom and dad." Another student said, "When I went off to college, I decided to keep the same curfew rules my mom had for me in high school. I felt she probably knew what was best for me, and I didn't want to ignore her advice."

Godly parents want the best for their children. Not disappointing or disregarding them is an honorable response by children. Good parents also intentionally place their children in challenging circumstances or refuse their request to bail them out when something becomes difficult. They say, "This will be good for you." Many parents today spend too much time shielding their children from any hardship. Wise parents allow their children to go through challenging, sometimes painful, experiences. Wise parents know that children mature by being supported while they work through problems rather than being encouraged to run away from them.

God is like that with his leaders. He may call you to a difficult place. You may be discouraged, thinking you are a failure or God has forgotten you. Neither is true. God has called you not only to work through you but also in you. He is at work through your circumstances. Just like a child who bails out of tough circumstances, as a leader you can leave a tough situation too quickly before God finishes teaching you all you are supposed to learn from it.

Remember, a call from God lasts until a subsequent, superseding call occurs. A called person cannot simply leave when things get tough. Called men and women stay put until God calls them to another assignment. Ministry leaders must not leave difficult situations just because they are difficult. There are, however, appropriate times to walk away from a ministry position. For example, if you are asked to compromise your integrity, break the law, violate moral standards, or diverge from core doctrinal convictions, you should refuse—even if it means you must resign. Although these instances are rare, they do occur. Stand firm in tough times, but also be prepared to make the costly choice to stand up for what is right and walk away when necessary.

God's Call Infuses Appropriate Authority

God's call brings with it a sense of enabling authority or power. That scares some people. A few leaders have misused authority to become autocratic, the "thus says the Lord through me and only me" type of leaders. Actually, *leader* is not an accurate description of a person with that attitude. *Despot* is a better word. The fact that a few leaders have misused the power given ministry leaders does not negate the need for the appropriate, healthy use of authority by leaders.

When God calls a person to ministry leadership, the expectation is that God will work through that person in a unique or special way. Spiritual communities—churches or ministry organizations—treat called persons with deference and a sense of higher spiritual expectation. God's people expect God-called leaders to lead.

Called persons, particularly when they answer God's call to a specific ministry position, are also infused with the authority of the position. In my first meeting as president with the executive leaders of our seminary, I was the least experienced person in the room. Nonetheless, those leaders looked to me for leadership because of the authority of the office to which God had placed me. Likewise, young pastors are often surprised when men and women many years their senior look to them and ask, "What do you sense God wants us to do, Pastor?"

God's call to ministry leadership and to a specific ministry assignment is coupled with special authority or ability to influence people. It also comes with intuitive insight and spiritual direction from God about how to do ministry. A logical question follows: "Is God's call enough to empower me for the ministry?" Or put another way: "Because God has called me, shouldn't I trust him alone for the insight and ability to do his work?"This question relates to the first effect of being called: confidence. Is God's call all a person needs to have the confidence, authority, and insight for a lifetime of ministry?

Based on biblical examples and contemporary observation, the answer is no. God has a pattern, a life cycle common to most leaders in the Bible. He called them to ministry leadership, sent them through a training process, and then called them to a specific ministry assignment. This same pattern works for most leaders today. God calls ministry leaders, trains them, and then assigns them a leadership role. True, sometimes these phases overlap or occur in a different order, but all are essential for long-term effectiveness.

David was anointed a future king, but then he waited twenty years before assuming the throne. The disciples answered God's call from Jesus, and then they trained for three years to lead the early church. Paul was converted and then sent to Arabia for three years. Sometimes training comes prior to the call, as when God sent Moses to the desert for years of preparation before calling him through the burning bush. But even in that case, God still trained the person he called. The predominant pattern is: God calls persons to ministry leadership, sends them through training, and then assigns them a specific ministry to lead. A call to lead is always a call to prepare.

The intensive preparation phase is the stage younger leaders often want to skip. Leaders who skip this phase say, "God has called me. That's all I need." Sadly, that attitude ignores the biblical pattern of how God usually works and the experience of most effective leaders. Most effective leaders today were very intentional about their initial training for leadership and thereafter continually retrain to stay on the cutting edge.

Preparation for ministry leadership involves formal and informal processes; both are valid and necessary. The best case is for the two forms of training to be integrated and to build on each other. Informal training is the training a ministry leader receives by observing others, learning through trial leadership opportunities, reading and researching about ministry leadership, attending seminars or conferences, and learning from peers. All are valid ways to learn to lead. Every good leader does these things throughout his or her lifetime. Good leaders are lifelong learners.

But is informal training enough? Usually not. Leaders who depend on informal training often gravitate toward certain subjects, models, formats, and personalities. This results in an imbalanced approach to ministry—long on repeating the programs and approaches of others but short on innovation and contemporaneous creativity. Informal training needs the balance and perspective that more formal training provides.

Formal training usually involves entering a ministry leadership training program offered through a college, university, or seminary. These programs are helpful for several reasons:

- *Formal training makes you accountable to others.* This can motivate you to focus on learning, growing, and developing as a leader in ways you would not or could not do on your own.
- *Formal training stretches your thinking.* You will read books you might not otherwise choose, consider different viewpoints, and encounter new concepts and ideas to expand your understanding of ministry.
- *Formal training enlarges your worldview.* You will meet people from other cultures and learn from professors with widely varying backgrounds and experiences.
- *Formal training focuses on the theological and theoretical foundation for ministry.* This information is essential for sustaining lifelong ministry leader-

ship and preparing you for future challenges you can't anticipate but need to be prepared to meet.

- *Formal training, done well, also incorporates the on-the-job training that leaders need to practice the art of ministry leadership.* Our seminary, for example, requires one year of supervised, on-the-job ministry training incorporating a field mentor, spiritual director, and follower's evaluation of a student leader's growth. Many other schools have similar programs.
- *Formal training puts you in contact with people and resources you will draw on throughout your lifetime.* Your professors and peers turn into lifelong friends, mentors, coaches, and supporters.

Despite the advantages noted above, formal approaches to ministry training are sometimes criticized. Some common complaints include the following (with short responses to bring some perspective):

- *"Formal training takes too long."* Formal ministry training takes about as long as law school and less time than medical school. Would you want your attorney or physician to shortcut his or her training? We should not validate a shortcut method for training ministry leaders for eternal purposes.
- *"Formal training is out of date."* Formal ministry training focuses on the timeless theological and

theoretical foundations for ministry. Mastering these will help you analyze contemporary culture and ministry methods rather than be controlled by them or feel the need to always chase after the latest, greatest how-to seminar.

- *"Formal training costs too much."* Check seminary prices against graduate or professional school tuition, and you will be shocked. Formal ministry training is the least expensive of all major academic or professional disciplines.

- *"Formal training drains your spiritual passion."* Some schools might do this, but most do not. Passion will be harnessed and focused, not intentionally diminished by formal training. One student told me, "I've got the burning; now I need the learning." Putting these together—spiritual passion and practical scholarship—is a good description of the goal of quality formal ministerial training.

When God calls, he infuses power and authority for ministry leadership. When he assigns you to a specific leadership role, this gift is magnified. You can trust God to work through you with appropriate power. His work is always *his work* to do through you. But part of God's work is training you to be most useful and available to him. Find the balance between formal and informal training for ministry. Build a foundation for lifelong leadership, then remain a lifelong learner. But no matter how much you learn, always rest in God's power for your ministry.

God's Call Leads to Humility

God empowers you for ministry leadership through his call. He expects you to be trained for leadership, which involves both informal processes and perhaps earning one or more degrees. He calls you to leadership roles— some with prestigious and honorable titles like *pastor* or *missionary* or *professor*. All of this can lead to pride. After all, you may become a God-called, well-trained, highly placed leader in God's kingdom.

But all of this should prompt humility, not pride. God's call reminds you that you are what you are by his work and at his initiative. God bestows spiritual leadership. It is not achieved by creative effort or skillful invention. God's call reminds you that he is in charge of your life and ministry. God's call produces humility, not pride.

In 1 Corinthians 4:7 Paul asked, "Who makes you so superior? What do you have that you didn't receive? If, in fact, you did receive it, why do you boast as if you hadn't received it?" This is a great question for leaders to memorize and consider often. Your call to ministry does not make you superior to anyone. You received your call to ministry. Your ministry is a received ministry, not an achieved ministry. You have nothing to boast about. Your call to ministry leadership came from God, and God has enabled your positive response.

Allow God's call to give you confidence, aid your perseverance, infuse you with authority, and produce humility. Resist the temptation to feel pride in your call or in any position that results from your call. Receive your call as a gracious gift from God and let it have its full effect in your life—including humbling you as you fulfill your call as the leader God intends you to be.

The Call to Missions

CHAPTER 7

In these final two chapters, let's consider two of the primary calls God extends for a specific ministry assignment. God calls people to many specific ministry or missional leadership roles. He calls collegiate ministers, preschool directors, and Bible teachers. He calls people to lead ministries to the homeless, inner-city youth programs, and medical clinics. God calls to a myriad of specific leadership assignments, but the two most common categories are pastoral ministry and missionary service. Simply put, God calls pastors and missionaries.

One of the special ways God calls is the call to missions. This specific call usually comes after a person has already sensed a general call to ministry leadership. Often a person is called to ministry leadership and expresses a willingness to serve in a missionary role, including international missions. Then, through a process of training and growth, the missionary call becomes clear. Often this call comes in the context of a growing interest in a specific people group or geographic location. Many students come to seminary saying, "God has called me to ministry leadership, and I am open to God calling me to missions." That seems to be a frequent progression not only for seminary students but also for persons of all ages who ultimately experience God's call to missions.

The call to missions is one of the most misunderstood callings among Christians. People often misunderstand this call as an immediate mandate to move to another country. Although that may be part of this call (and often is), it is not the defining component. Also, a call to missions can be misunderstood because of how slowly it comes to fruition. It usually requires a slow, somewhat methodical fulfillment. Most mission boards require candidates to have training and experience prior to appointment. This takes time. Some missionaries have to raise their own financial support, which also takes time. The call to missions must almost always be confirmed by others since it involves appointment and/or financial support from an organization, church, or another group of believers. This also takes time. So, a call to missions is usually confirmed over time as a person moves step-by-step through an unfolding discovery process.

Paul was the most effective missionary in the early church. His call to missions and his mission work are summarized in the book of Acts, beginning in Acts 13. He wrote about his experiences in several of his letters to churches, particularly in Ephesians 3. His summary provides a good framework to properly understand the call to missions and what it might mean in your life.

A Call to Missions Begins at Conversion

The foundation for a call to missions is the common experience of all believers who are commissioned for mission service at their conversion. Paul wrote, "I was made a servant of this gospel by the gift of God's grace that was given to me by the working of His power" (Eph. 3:7). As a servant of the gospel, Paul was a preacher, teacher, church planter, and writer. All of that describes his missionary work.

The phrase "by the gift of God's grace" alludes to Paul's conversion experience. In this same letter he wrote, "By grace you are saved through faith, and this is not from yourselves; it is God's gift" (Eph. 2:8). Paul described his conversion as a work of God's grace, a gift from God. He clearly traced the beginning of his missionary work to his conversion experience.

God commissions every believer as "a servant of this gospel" simultaneous to his or her conversion. When you were saved, you were commissioned to missionary service. You were commissioned to a missional lifestyle, to being an on-mission Christian. You may be thinking, *Really? I didn't know that was part of my conversion.* There are many results of your conversion you probably didn't know occurred at the time. Several of these were discussed earlier in the context of your universal call to Christian service. Just because you didn't know these things occurred doesn't mean they didn't happen.

We often enter commitments without full knowledge of the implications. For example, students sign up for classes without really knowing what the professor will require. After a few weeks they are searching for a way to change their schedules. New homeowners are sometimes surprised with the repair and maintenance required by their purchase—the house looked so nice when the realtor showed it!

Perhaps the best example is marriage. A couple says "I do" with little idea what they are really doing. Over the next few months they begin to learn about the person they married. Many surprises ensue! When people marry, they are committing to what they know as well as to what they don't know about the person they are marrying.

So it is with your conversion. When you were saved, you were commissioned to be on mission. In that sense every believer is called to missions, to living a missional lifestyle. Some, of course, are later called to ministry leadership and then to missions as a specific life calling. Still, the genesis of the missionary call, conversion, is common to all believers.

A Call to Missions Is to People, Not Places

Paul was a traveling man. He made three mission trips—plus a trip to Rome as a prisoner, which could also be considered a mission trip considering how aggressively he evangelized sailors, guards, and Roman leaders. Paul went to and through major cities and many provinces during his missionary career, but when he summarized his call to missions, he referenced people rather than a geographic locale.

Paul wrote, "This grace was given to me . . . to proclaim to the Gentiles the incalculable riches of the Messiah" (Eph. 3:8). Paul identified the Gentiles—not a city, province, or country—as the object of his mission. *Gentiles* is a broad, generic term for non-Jews. Paul's call was expressed in terms of people, not places. In modern missionary terminology, the Gentiles were the people group (albeit a very large people group) he felt called to reach.

The missionary call is a call to people. It is a call to identify and reach certain people whom God places on your heart. The question to clarify your missional call is not "Am I called?" The better question is "Whom am I called to reach?" Borrowing and building on the idea expressed in Paul's call, you might ask, "Who are my Gentiles?"

Some will answer this question with people in their neighborhood or community. Others will answer it cross-culturally, requiring relocation to a different country or culture. When God calls you to reach your Gentiles, he expects you to structure or restructure your life to accomplish his mission. Doing this may require a geographic change, but again, the relocation is a result of the call, not the call itself.

A couple told me they were called to reach Vietnamese people. They applied to a mission board and were accepted for service in Germany. This really puzzled me. "Why Germany when you are called to Vietnam?" I asked. "We aren't called to Vietnam," they replied. "We are called to reach Vietnamese people. There are more than one hundred thousand Vietnamese service workers in the German city where we are being sent." This couple had a clear understanding of their call. They were called to reach Vietnamese people, not to the spot on the map called Vietnam.

Similarly, another couple moved to Brazil to work with several million German-speaking, German-heritage Brazilians. They lived in Brazil, but it seemed more like Germany. In the twenty-first century, traditional borders are melting as people migrate around the world. Answering God's call to missions is answering his call to reach people who may or may not be in their traditional locations.

Another couple came to seminary with a call to reach Mandarin-speaking Chinese people. They immediately joined the Mandarin Chinese church in a nearby city to begin fulfilling their call. Some people claim they are called to reach a certain people group but will not involve themselves in reaching immigrants from that group living nearby. These people are confused. A missionary call is not a junket. It is a commission to reach people. A cross-cultural missionary call means you get started *now,* not when you move to another country. Most major cities are multi-cultural stew pots, affording the opportunity to immediately answer God's call to missionary service without moving to another country. These are ideal locations to test your call and improve your skills while you are training to work in another country or cultural setting.

Sometimes the missionary call takes a different form. Rather than just thinking cross-culturally, the answer to "Who are my Gentiles?" may lead you on mission to a people group very close to you. God most often sends us on mission to the people we already know. He sends us on mission to schoolmates, work associates, neighborhood friends, or fellow club members. When you ask God, "Who are my Gentiles?" do not be surprised if the answer is someone, or some group, you know well.

Too many Christians overlook the obvious mission field around them. For example, our children were heavily involved in youth sports. All three of our children played multiple sports through high school. We spent thousands of hours at practices, games, team parties, and traveling to and from sporting events for about fifteen years. We never used this as an excuse to be too busy to share our faith. We used these relationships as the conduit for sharing our faith.

Most of the people our family has been influential in leading to faith in Jesus have been friends—players, coaches, umpires, and parents—we met through youth sports. We shared our faith, naturally but intentionally, with sports friends throughout the years. Some of these witnessing relationships took a long time to develop. But eventually, living with people through all kinds of life experiences, we were able to see some of our friends become Christians.

Although your mission field may be all around you, you still may need to create unique venues to accomplish your mission. My oldest son started a Fellowship of Christian Athletes ministry to crystallize his outreach to fellow athletes. My other son started a Christian Club at a public high school—not for Christian fellowship but as a discussion venue allowing unbelievers to learn about the Christian worldview. Intentional, creative strategies are often required to reach out to people around you.

A call to missions is primarily a call to people, not places. A call to missions is a call to communicate the gospel to people. God calls most believers to reach the people in their circle of influence. That is your primary mission field. You can do that through relationships or through creating intentional strategies for communicating the gospel.

While all believers share a missional responsibility, some are specifically called to cross-cultural mission work. When they ask, "Who are my Gentiles?" the answer is another cultural, ethnic, or language group. Obeying this call usually involves geographic change—moving across town or around the world. While this is the traditional view of a call to missions, the relocation is more a by-product of the call than the essence of the call itself.

A Call to Missions Involves You in God's Eternal Purpose

Joining God on mission to others unites you with God's eternal purpose. Paul wrote that both his call and the wonder of the gospel were "according to [God's] purpose of the ages" (Eph. 3:11). In this context Paul also wrote of God's mystery, the manifold wisdom of his redemptive plan. Revealing and explaining that plan to all humankind was God's eternal purpose. Paul found his eternal purpose by joining God in that process. You can do the same as you share the gospel with people.

Think about how temporary life is. For most of us, life is full of daily duties, such as answering the phone, changing diapers, mowing the lawn, going to meetings, and fighting traffic. Even the more purposeful, meaningful aspects of life such as family activities and job successes are temporary. Much of what we do does not last more than a few days, much less our lifetime.

However, joining God on mission to the world, to your part of his world, is different. It is your opportunity to join God in doing something eternal. You get to invest yourself in people. By telling them the gospel, you reveal God's purpose for them. When they believe the gospel, they receive eternal life with God. They may live many more years, but their eternal destiny is secured.

Doing something that lasts forever brings new meaning to life. You have purpose rather than existence. You share in God's plan for the ages—sending Jesus to redeem people and to create the church for a relationship with him. My most significant ministry investment was to help start a new church in Oregon. Every time we visit the church, we are reminded of the eternal results our efforts have achieved and will yet achieve. We helped put in motion a movement of reaching new people with the gospel. Winning people to Jesus and helping organize a church to continue the process have eternal results and rewards.

A call to missions is a call to God's eternal purpose. Since your conversion, you have shared this call. Are you living it? If so, thank God for inviting you into his eternal purpose. If not, ask God, "Who are my Gentiles?" and then get busy taking the gospel to them. As people around you begin to be saved, you will sense an eternal satisfaction that comes from seeing this happen. If your Gentiles are part of another culture or a people group who have never heard the gospel, you may start an eternal chain reaction lasting centuries. What a privilege!

A Call to Missions Requires Sacrifice

Answering God's call to missions, particularly to a cross-cultural assignment that requires a major relocation, involves sacrifice. Paul wrote of his sacrifice, telling the Ephesians "not to be discouraged over my afflictions on your behalf, for they are your glory" (Eph. 3:13). *Afflictions* is a strong word. Paul had suffered physically to get the gospel to them. He wrote to them from a Roman prison, his life soon to end because of his missionary work. A call to missions involves sacrifice, sometimes even a life-giving sacrifice.

Larry and Jean Elliot, along with two team members, gave the ultimate sacrifice as missionaries. They were some of the first Christian workers in Iraq after the Saddam Hussein regime was overthrown. Larry and Jean, along with David and Carrie McDonnall and Karen Watson, were searching for sites to establish fresh-water wells when their car was strafed. All but Carrie were killed. These men and women gave their lives trying to get clean water—and then Living Water—to the Iraqi people. Carrie survived, but she lives with the loss of her husband and friends.

These martyrs join a long line of mostly unknown believers who have given their lives for the expansion of God's kingdom. They died willingly, making the ultimate sacrifice to get the gospel to as many people as possible. Similarly, missionaries who serve thirty or forty years on the field, only to return with broken health and very limited financial resources, have made a similar, though less dramatic, sacrifice. They, too, have given their lives for the gospel.

Answering a call to missions, particularly in the traditional sense of international missionary service, requires sacrifice. You will sacrifice time with your family, missing occasions like holiday celebrations and memorial services for family members. Comforts of home must be forsaken. Before we left on a recent trip to visit a missionary group, one person e-mailed, "Bring a small jar of peanut butter if you can. What a treat it would be!" Wal-Mart may be almost everywhere, but none have been built yet in the jungle where those missionaries are serving. Even a jar of peanut butter was a special treat.

Stories of sacrifice inspire us. One of my favorites is from the book *The Cry of the Kalahari* by Mark and Delia Owens.[2] Here is an edited excerpt that describes their sacrifice.

2. Mark and Delia Owens, *The Cry of the Kalahari* (Boston: Mariner Books, 1992), 3–4.

Delia and I met in class at the University of Georgia, and it didn't take us long to find out that we shared the same goal. By the end of the semester we knew that when we went to Africa, it would have to be together.

We decided to take a leave from the university and earn the money needed to finance the expedition. Once a site had been chosen, we thought someone would surely grant us the funds to continue.

But after six months of teaching, we had saved nothing. I switched jobs and began operating a stone-quarry crusher while Delia worked at odd jobs. At the end of another six months, we had saved $4900, plus money for airfares to Johannesburg. But it was still not enough.

Trying desperately to raise more, we piled everything we owned—stereo, radio, television, fishing rod and reel, pots and pans—into our station wagon and drove to the quarry one morning, just as the men were coming off the night shift. I auctioned it all away, including the car, for $1100.

A year after we were married, we boarded a plane with two backpacks, two sleeping bags, one pup tent, a small cooking kit, a camera, one change of clothes each and $6000. It was all we had.

Why would the Owenses make this kind of sacrifice? To study the brown hyena! That's right, the brown hyena! This is not a story of a young missionary couple—it's the story of two young researchers willing to sacrifice to advance scientific knowledge of large carnivores in the Kalahari desert. While their example is inspiring, it is also humbling.

Many Christians complain about the slightest inconvenience. Where is our willingness to sacrifice? Radical environmentalists, homosexual activists, and religious fanatics all around the world are giving their lives to advance their causes. Even more should be expected of us, who claim to have the message of eternal life for the world.

A call to missions, however it is expressed through your life, will require sacrifice. It will cost you time, energy, resources, and personal comfort to get the gospel to others. That is true if you are taking the gospel down the street, across your state, or around the world. A call to missions, your call to missions, will require sacrifice.

Yet like Paul, you will hardly notice the difficulty. You will say, as he told the Ephesians, "My afflictions . . . are your glory" (Eph. 3:13). Whatever sacrifice we might make pales before the joy of knowing we have been instrumental in helping people become followers of Jesus.

So, who are your Gentiles? Whom has God called you to reach with the gospel? As you answer that question, be prepared to make the lifestyle changes necessary to fulfill your missionary call. It may be as simple as creating an intentional strategy to share your faith with friends at work or as dramatic as moving to a different country (with the language and cultural adjustments that mandates). Whatever is required to answer your missionary call, do it and enjoy the eternal fulfillment that comes from being involved in God's ultimate purpose.

The Call to Pastoral Ministry

CHAPTER 8

A call to pastoral ministry is another special way God calls to a specific ministry assignment. The phrase *pastoral ministry* can refer to anyone who is called to pastoral leadership in the church. This can include the person sometimes called senior pastor or lead pastor or any of the various kinds of pastors or associate pastors in churches today. While God calls to many pastoral roles, the focus of this chapter is on God calling a person to be the pastor— the person with the general spiritual oversight of a local church.

You may not think this chapter applies to you, particularly if you are fairly certain you are not called to be a pastor. Keep reading for two reasons. First, you may be mistaken. God may want you to be a pastor, and you need to further investigate this kind of call. Second, if you are not a pastor, you will have a pastor. Or, you may be involved in selecting a pastor for your church in the future. Either way, understanding the call to pastoral ministry is important for whatever future relationship you may have to the pastoral office in your church.

The call to pastoral ministry—or the call to preach, as it was sometimes called in a previous generation—was for many years the standard way to express God's call. This is no longer the case. Today, God's general call to ministry is usually understood as a call to ministry leadership instead of a particular role or office. Like a call to missions, a call to pastoral leadership often emerges from a general call to ministry leadership.

This shift in how God's call has been described is not intended to diminish the importance of a call to pastoral ministry or to preaching. It is, instead, an attempt to understand God's call in a more general sense, thus including the many different kinds of ministry leadership roles in God's kingdom today. This book embraces a progressive understanding of God's call, moving from a general call to ministry leadership and then to a specific call to a role or assignment. Nevertheless, it is important to consider the call to pastoral ministry as a unique, necessary, and significant call from God. The pastoral call must be lifted up as a significant leadership call among the varied options in the kingdom.

An alarming issue today is the decreasing percentage of men who attend seminary with a focused commitment to become pastors. While many problems with pastors and pastoral leadership (immorality, fiscal irresponsibility, doctrinal errors, etc.) are evident in the church, the most distressing problem for the future may be a shortage of pastors. Part of solving this problem is elevating the pastoral call to its appropriate role and importance.

This chapter addresses two aspects of pastoral calling that, when properly understood, underscore the importance of this kind of call. First, we will look at the uniqueness of the call to pastoral ministry. The pastoral office, along with the qualities and qualifications for those called to pastoral ministry, is the most clearly defined church leadership role in the New Testament. This enables us to understand many different dimensions of this kind of call. Second, in this chapter we will address the common reasons people who are called to pastoral ministry resist this call. These may include some of your concerns. Our discussion of these two aspects of pastoral calling will be based on the description of the pastoral office in 1 Timothy 3:1–7.

The Pastoral Call Is a High Calling

The pastoral office is a "noble work" to which a person "aspires" (1 Tim. 3:1). This lofty language describes the dignity, honor, and prestige attached to pastoral ministry. The office itself, regardless of the person holding it, is significant, elevating the status of the occupant rather than the other way around.

Pastoral ministry is a worthy calling, though not everyone agrees. When I was in college, the vice president of a multinational company asked me about my career plans. I said, "I am going to be a pastor." He replied, "Why would you want to waste your life doing that?" He thought nothing could be more irrelevant than leading a church, having the care of souls, and representing the gospel to a community. The Bible has a different view. The pastoral office is honorable and worth giving your life for.

African-American churches often elevate the pastoral office in tangible ways. In many churches there is one pulpit for the pastor to speak from and another smaller podium for all others to use. A friend took a youth group to Los Angeles for a mission trip in Watts. The group visited Mt. Zion Baptist Church to hear Dr. E. V. Hill preach. After the service, one of the boys considering a call to pastoral ministry wanted to have his picture taken while standing behind the pulpit. As he neared the pulpit, a deacon intercepted him and kindly (but firmly) said, "Young man, please step away from the pulpit. Only Dr. Hill stands there." The pulpit in that church is a powerful symbol of the office, the man who occupies it, and the church's respect for both. While every culture expresses this understanding differently, all should find ways to honor the importance of pastoral ministry.

Pastoral leadership is also important because of who is being led. The church is "the administration of the mystery hidden for ages in God who created all things" (Eph. 3:9). God reveals his "multi-faceted wisdom . . . through the church to the rulers and authorities in the heavens" (Eph. 3:10). The church is God's ultimate prize, his final "purpose of the ages" (Eph. 3:11). When you consider the exalted position of the church in God's plan, you will understand the high office pastors have. The President of the United States is more important than the president of the Rotary Club because of the power, influence, and scope of who and what he leads. Pastors lead God's most precious creation and possession—the church! The importance of their office is magnified by whom they lead.

Some people in today's society diminish the importance of the church, considering it irrelevant and passé. Ineffective, spiritually cold churches might confirm this impression. Be careful about jumping on this bandwagon! God will sustain his church. He will sustain an organized, visible expression of the church until the end of time. The church may need reform, may take new forms, and may experience major changes in our generation, but its predicted demise is greatly overstated. God promises that his church will survive until the end of time—then for all time with him. That church, like any organization needs leaders—pastors who respond to God's call and assume this high office.

The Pastoral Call Is a Character Calling

Most descriptions of pastors in the Bible relate to their character, not their skills or training. Paul described a pastor as "above reproach . . . self-controlled, sensible, respectable, hospitable . . . not addicted to wine, not a bully but gentle, not quarrelsome, not greedy . . . [with] a good reputation among outsiders" (1 Tim. 3:2–7). These character qualities raise a high standard of personal deportment and emotional control.

Pastors are required to be examples of Christian character and Christian character development. The first phrase, "above reproach," is a daunting standard. Pastors are to live in such a way that others can emulate their attitudes and behavior. Frankly, this is one of the reasons some people resist the call to pastoral ministry or want to interpret their call in more generic (and less stressful) terms. They simply don't want the pressure of being a moral example in their church and community.

Some people caution against elevating pastors and expecting them to live exemplary lives. The Bible indicates otherwise. Pastors are expected to live differently, to be above reproach. This does not mean pastors should be placed on the "perfection pedestal." No pastor is perfect, but neither is he expected to be by any biblical or reasonable standard. Part of modeling Christian character, of being above reproach, is modeling the transparency to confess sin, be forgiven, and take responsibility for the consequences. Although pastors are not expected to be perfect, they are expected to live circumspectly as examples to their church and community. One friend has a small plaque that says: "Others may; I cannot." It's a simple reminder that he is called to live differently, that what others may do he simply can't do and still remain above reproach.

Another aspect of this character calling is that pastoral ministry will test your character. Being a pastor is a tough job! Pastoral leadership is a crucible for character development. God uses the role as a refining fire to smelt out impurities. Pastoral ministry is also challenging because pastors work with people as shepherds of a flock. And some sheep bite! Several character qualities, such as "self-controlled . . . hospitable . . . not a bully but gentle, not quarrelsome, not greedy . . . a good reputation among outsiders" (1 Tim. 3:2–7), are best developed and demonstrated in relationship with difficult people. If you answer God's call to pastoral ministry, prepare to have some challenging times of personal growth as you lead people. God will use these experiences, and you will ultimately be grateful for them, but they are painful when they occur. Being a pastor requires exemplary character, and the role will test your character.

The Pastoral Call Is a Family Calling

Pastoral ministry, like many other roles in ministry, often involves the entire family. Paul acknowledged this fact when he wrote that a pastor must be "the husband of one wife . . . [and] one who manages his own household competently, having his children under control with all dignity" (1 Tim. 3:2, 4). The focus on these passages is usually on analyzing "husband of one wife" and clarifying what Paul meant by "under control." While those discussions are important, they are not our focus as they relate to this kind of call.

The overarching point of these phrases from Scripture is that a pastoral calling is a family calling. There is no escaping the reality that a pastor's family is significantly involved in his work. Some men reject their call to pastoral ministry because of fear that it will harm their family. Pastors must take precautions to preserve their family's identity and each person's participation in the church without inappropriate outside pressure that negatively impacts the family. But it is very difficult to lead a church while keeping your family entirely isolated from your pastoral responsibilities and function.

A pastor's wife must be supportive of his call. Her support can take many forms, and stereotypes must be avoided. If a pastor's wife is resistant to his being in pastoral ministry, he will not last long. Similarly, a pastor's children must be taught that they have been born to parents who share a pastoral call and, in appropriate ways, God intends for them to share and enjoy that environment. Knowing all that is involved in their father's role, God creates the children born into a pastoral family and places them in that setting.

One young man resisted his call to pastoral ministry because he didn't want his children to grow up with his serving in a pastoral role. He had heard the "war stories" about how hard it is to be part of a pastor's family, and he believed the stories without really analyzing what he was hearing. There *are* some hard things about growing up in a pastoral family. But there are also hard things about growing up in a physician's family, a plumber's family, a politician's family—and in every other kind of family.

On a more positive note, there are also some special blessings a pastor's family gets to enjoy. These are overlooked when people focus only on the challenges or problems. Here are some benefits our family experienced throughout our years in pastoral ministry:

- *Your family gets to go to work with you and see what you do.* When I left pastoral ministry to work for the denomination, my preschool son asked, "What does Daddy do now?" He felt a great loss in not seeing his father do ministry and sharing in it weekly.

- *Your family benefits from your flexible work schedule.* As a pastor, I was often the only father present for midday school functions. In addition, as I traveled to preach at conferences or other engagements, my children sometimes traveled with me, going places many of their friends never visited.
- *Your family gets to know, on a more personal basis, the best people on earth—church people!* Sure, sometimes they can be difficult, but most of the time, church friends—surrogate aunts, uncles, and grandparents—and fellow pastors are the very best people in the world. When I had cancer, church people rallied around our family in remarkable ways. Our children have never forgotten the love they were shown by so many who cared for them during those frightening days.
- *Your family gets to see God at work.* Your family, even though you are discreet and honor confidentiality, knows more details about how God is changing people than the typical church member does. They see God at work, up close and personal.
- *Your family will get to know other Christian leaders* (like guest speakers in your church) more personally than the average church member ever will.

These are just some of the benefits of being in a pastoral family. A pastor's family is part of his ministry. If you are called to pastoral ministry, celebrate the blessings of being in ministry with your family around you. Don't shy away from this call based on misplaced or overstated concerns for your family. And whatever you do, don't use your family as an excuse to reject God's call to pastoral ministry.

A Pastoral Call Is a Community Calling

Pastors have the opportunity to spiritually shepherd and impact their entire community. Paul recognized this influence by emphasizing that pastors "must have a good reputation among outsiders" (1 Tim. 3:7). After serving in a community for several years, it was not unusual for people to introduce me to friends as "my pastor" even though they had never once attended my church. When you work in the community, make a spiritual impact at community events, and serve the community's spiritual needs, people come to think of you as their pastor.

When a respected pastor has long tenure, he can have a significant community impact. Unfortunately, the reverse is also true. When a pastor sins morally or ethically, his failure becomes a community issue. Because pastors have community influence, these sins damage the reputation of the church and Christianity in general. Sometimes the stain lasts a long time. Once when I asked for directions to a certain church, I was told, "Oh, that's the church where the pastor killed his wife in the parsonage." Although it was true, it had also happened more than fifteen years before. A pastoral calling is a community calling, a stewardship that must be protected and nurtured as part of the opportunity God gives pastors to impact the culture.

Pastors, because of their calling and office, are recognized community leaders. They can use their influence for good. Their sins can have a disproportionately negative impact. The pastoral calling is a call to community service and responsibility. If you are called to pastoral ministry, honor the office and guard its integrity. Make sure you live above reproach and bring honor to your church, community, and Lord through your leadership example.

The call to pastoral ministry is a high calling. The spiritual leadership of a church, any church, is an awe-inspiring responsibility. If you are sensing a call to ministry, investigate to determine whether it is a call to *pastoral* ministry. God is still calling pastors, and he needs the best and brightest to lead his church. Despite what was once said to me, giving your life as a pastor is not a waste of time. It is an investment in God's most cherished possession— the church!

Don't limit God's work in your life by refusing to consider his calling to be a pastor. It's a tough calling— but worth it as you obey God and experience his pleasure as a pastor.

Continuing the Conversation

Writing this book was an attempt to help you clarify God's call in your life. Having a conversation with you would have been more enjoyable. Talking on our patio or at a coffee shop would have allowed for dialogue, questions, and better communication. You would have taught me new things, and we would have reached some fresh mutual understandings.

Alas, those conversations are not likely to happen. But if they did, I would ask you some of the following questions to guide our conversation. Determining God's call can't be reduced to a questionnaire or a checklist. Nonetheless, working through thought-provoking questions with a friend or mentor can help clarify your thinking. Use the following questions to continue working toward understanding God's call in your life. Consider talking through them with a spiritual guide you trust.

God has called you to Christian service. He may be calling you to ministry leadership or to a specific ministry assignment. God may be calling you right now. Or not! Either way, settling this issue will liberate you for future service and will enable you to freely serve God with reckless abandon. Nothing will be more fulfilling than knowing and doing God's will concerning the issue of call.

Questions for Reflection on God's Call

1. Do you agree with the definition of God's call (see p. 8)? Why or why not? What part of it connects with you and clarifies your understanding of call?

2. Are you fulfilling God's universal call for all believers to Christian service? If not, why not? How do you need to improve or change in this area?

3. Have you had (or are you now experiencing) God's general call to ministry leadership?

4. Do you understand the difference between the call to Christian service (for all believers) and the call to ministry leadership (for some believers)? How does your sense of vocational call fit into this model?

5. Do you understand the different ways God calls? Do you agree that all are valid, equal, and supernatural? Have you experienced any of these?

6. Do you believe God can call you? Have you been using any excuses to disqualify yourself from being called? How will you change your thinking about these issues?

7. As you process the potential of God's call in your life, how do you evaluate the following areas: inner peace, confirmation of others, joy in ministry, effectiveness in ministry, and realistic expectations about the ministry?

8. Do you agree that God's call can give you confidence and perseverance? How do you feel about God giving authority through his call? Does this reality produce humility in you?

9. Do you think formal training is helpful for a God-called person? Why or why not? Does your life-long learning plan include both formal and informal training?

10. How do you understand the call to missions? Do you know who your "Gentiles" are? Will missionary work among those people require a geographic or cultural relocation for you?

11. Are you called to pastoral ministry? Are you sure? Have you really considered this option?

12. If your call is clear, are you obeying God? What do you need to do to obey God's call to ministry leadership or to a specific ministry assignment?